Competitive Taekwondo

Master Yong Sup Kil
Kil's Taekwondo Centers

Human Kinetics

Library of Congress Cataloging-in-Publication Data

Kil, Yong Sup.
    Competitive taekwondo / Master Yong Sup Kil.
        p.   cm.
    Includes index.
    ISBN-13: 978-0-7360-5870-4 (soft cover)
    ISBN-10: 0-7360-5870-2 (soft cover)
    1. Tae kwon do.   I. Title.
    GV1114.9.K52   2006
    796.815'3--dc22

                                2006004463

ISBN-10: 0-7360-5870-2
ISBN-13: 978-0-7360-5870-4

Developmental Editor: Cynthia McEntire; **Assistant Editor:** Scott Hawkins; **Copyeditor:** Alisha Jeddeloh; **Proofreader:** Erin Cler; **Indexer:** Dan Connolly; **Graphic Designer:** Nancy Rasmus; **Graphic Artist:** Sandra Meier; **Photo Manager:** Dan Wendt; **Cover Designer:** Keith Blomberg; **Photographer (cover):** © Javier Soriano/AFP/Getty Images; **Photographers (interior):** Amanda Mays, Tom Rossman, and Kevin MacRitchie unless otherwise noted; **Art Manager and Illustrator:** Kareema McLendon-Foster; **Printer:** United Graphics

Human Kinetics books are available at special discounts for bulk purchase. Special editions or book excerpts can also be created to specification. For details, contact the Special Sales Manager at Human Kinetics.

Printed in the United States of America

10   9   8   7   6   5   4   3   2   1

Human Kinetics
Web site: www.HumanKinetics.com

United States: Human Kinetics
P.O. Box 5076
Champaign, IL 61825-5076
800-747-4457
e-mail: humank@hkusa.com

Canada: Human Kinetics
475 Devonshire Road Unit 100
Windsor, ON N8Y 2L5
800-465-7301 (in Canada only)
e-mail: orders@hkcanada.com

Europe: Human Kinetics
107 Bradford Road
Stanningley
Leeds LS28 6AT, United Kingdom
+44 (0) 113 255 5665
e-mail: hk@hkeurope.com

Australia: Human Kinetics
57A Price Avenue
Lower Mitcham, South Australia 5062
08 8277 1555
e-mail: liaw@hkaustralia.com

New Zealand: Human Kinetics
Division of Sports Distributors NZ Ltd.
P.O. Box 300 226 Albany
North Shore City
Auckland
0064 9 448 1207
e-mail: info@humankinetics.co.nz

To my mother,
for her spiritual strength and loving heart
in raising eight wonderful children.

Contents

Foreword

Taekwondo is a growing martial art all over the world. Its increasing popularity is evidenced by the 60 million students of this martial art in 179 countries. International competition continues to advance through events such as the World Championships and the Olympic Games.

Competitive Taekwondo, written by Master Yong Sup Kil and endorsed by the World Taekwondo Federation, contains the insight of a veteran athlete and coach. The book covers the theoretical background of the match, training methods for athletes, kicks, steps, tactics, and sparring strategies. The variety of training covered in the book will expedite a better understanding of taekwondo and give readers a competitive edge.

This is a good guidebook for trainees, athletes, and coaches who have a keen desire to understand taekwondo. It is my sincere wish this wonderful martial art continues to inspire all those who seek knowledge of the sport.

Chungwon Choue, PhD
President
World Taekwondo Federation

Acknowledgments

In the odyssey of writing this book, many friends and colleagues helped bring this project to fruition. I would like to acknowledge their loyalty and friendship.

First and foremost, I want to thank Master Jong Chul Lee, Korean national champion 1973 to 1980, 1988 Olympic coach for the Mexican national team, head coach of the 2003 U.S. national collegiate team to the Summer World Universiade games, and professor of martial arts at the University of Bridgeport, Connecticut.

For technical advice and his support and strong influence in my life, I thank my dear brother, Grand Master Sang Sup Kil, an international sport leader; Grand Master Kwang Sup Kil, my brother, friend, and colleague; Master Ali Koubeissi, vice president of the Michigan TKD Association and head coach of the Michigan TKD team; Master Young Seoung Kim, Korean national champion and U.S. national and college team coach; Master Jae Ho Kim, Korean national champion and U.S. national and college team coach; Professor Jun Chul Yoon, Korean champion and U.S. national and college team coach; Master Eric Sang Kim and Master Chang Kil Kim, friends and colleagues; and Kil's branch instructors Bill and Tammy Walker and Jack Kittinger.

Special thanks to Denise Delleree, second dan, for her patience and understanding as my editing assistant. Without her help and technical knowledge, this book would not have been completed.

Thanks to Thomas Rossman, Tom Mays, Amanda Mays, and Kevin R. MacRitchie.

Thanks to the sparring partners (and my students) who helped individualize and break down the movements of taekwondo—Benjamin Kil, Kelly Verpoort, and Juan Perez.

Thanks to my family, especially my mom and my wife, for supporting my dream.

And finally, thanks to Cynthia McEntire for walking me through this endeavor and to the staff at Human Kinetics for believing in me.

Introduction

Taekwondo is my life! My life started prematurely, which gave my mother and father great concern. As I grew and became healthy, my parents enrolled me in taekwondo to build my body and mind. At five years of age, I had already watched two older brothers grow through the teachings of a taekwondo master in Korea. Starting out a little smaller in this world did not diminish my motivation to be the best.

My training continues to this day. I have been directly involved in national and international competitions throughout my career. Over the years I have made use of many writings, manuals, and philosophies of taekwondo for information, expertise, and inspiration in my technique. However, as I became more involved in coaching, refereeing, and, most recently, teaching taekwondo at the university level, it became apparent to me that there was a great need for a book focusing on competition. Of course, there are many martial arts books on the market, but they are directed toward the fundamental aspects of the sport.

This void in martial arts literature led me to write this book. Even though my knowledge and experience are extensive, I am sure there are omissions of strategy and technique, and others in the field of taekwondo may have greater expertise in certain areas. My goal is to provide basic guidelines and suggestions for training and competition.

The task of putting words on paper to describe the movements of an athlete is difficult at best. There are so many nuances to the art of taekwondo and its rhythm, strength, and grace that sometimes it feels as if a disservice has been done to the athletes of the sport. However, my heart and spirit are pure in intention. My desire is for this text to become a guide for coaches, instructors, masters, and athletes everywhere who love taekwondo as much as I do.

UNDERSTANDING TAEKWONDO

Taekwondo is a unique martial art that began more than 2,000 years ago as a system of defense for aristocrats. Over the centuries these self-defense methods evolved into specific skills and a philosophy that found their way into the daily life of the common people. As its popularity grew, taekwondo became more competitive. Yaksok gyorugi (promise sparring), a form of taekwondo interaction with drills, became widespread and was developed as a sport. However, yaksok gyorugi did not satisfy the competitive drive of the athletes because it lacked the spontaneous use of skill and independent action. Over time the sport become more organized, and in 1962 the Korean Taesudo Association, the Korean Taekwondo Association, and the Korean Amateur Sports Association joined forces. The goal of building a national Korean sport started to take shape.

Taekwondo nurtures the mind and body by creating harmony between physical and mental training through the use of the hands and feet. The word *taekwondo* delivers the full meaning of the martial art. *Tae* stands for basic kicks, including kicks in the air. The word *kwon* means "fist that blocks and punches." Finally, the word *do* translates into a philosophy of conduct that is cultivated through discipline and training of body and mind.

Although students can build physical strength and skills under the tutelage of a taekwondo master, it is the philosophical foundation of taekwondo that makes the student a whole athlete. The spirit of taekwondo centers on integrity, self-control, indomitable spirit, perseverance, humility, and courtesy. These tenets are the foundation of training in and out of the dojang (school) for those who embrace the art.

Taekwondo is a unique sport in that the master and student forge a symbiotic relationship. Whereas a coach and athlete will train and compete as a team, in taekwondo there is a sense of honor and respect for the master that goes deeper than the sport itself. Trainees quickly learn the deep-seated culture of respect and courtesy practiced in taekwondo. Self-confidence and achievement are gained by persevering through repetitive training with resoluteness and indomitable spirit. Correct sporting behavior requires accepting the win or loss of a game in the spirit of fair play. When the proper attitude toward winning or losing becomes more important than the result of a match, an athlete is born again as a man or woman of taekwondo.

Today the sport of international taekwondo consists of basic motions (a set of standard stances), yaksok gyorugi, jayu gyorugi (free sparring or contest without preset rules and with spontaneous actions), breaking, and the art of self-defense.

Formal competition is composed of three elements: poomse, sparring, and breaking. Poomse (forms) are combinations of basic movements such as blocking, punching, and kicking. The athlete demonstrates skill by quickly evading attack from the left and right sides, following imaginary poomse lines with speed, accuracy, rhythm, balance, and concentration. Poomse teach a fighter to respond quickly to constantly changing motion. Skills developed in poomse provide a strong foundation for sparring competition.

COMPETITIVE DEVELOPMENT

Even though martial arts have been around for more than 2,000 years, only in the last 30 years have they evolved into organized, competitive sports recognized by the international athletic community. On May 28, 1973, the World Taekwondo Federation (WTF) was founded, and soon after many countries around the world established taekwondo associations. In 1975 the WTF became a member of the International Amateur Sports Federation (IASF), which further solidified the presence of competitive taekwondo on the international sport scene.

In May of 1980, the International Olympic Committee (IOC) recognized taekwondo as an international sport. In 1988 and 1992, taekwondo was chosen as a demonstration event at the Olympic Games, and in 2000 and 2004 it was included as an official Olympic event.

The three major arenas of competitive taekwondo are official international taekwondo competitions, international goodwill competitions, and combined sports games. These are all official international games.

Official international taekwondo competitions include the World Taekwondo Championship; the World Junior Taekwondo Championship; the World University Taekwondo Championship, sponsored by International University Sports Federation (FISU); the World International Servicemen Taekwondo Championship; and the World Cup.

In international goodwill taekwondo competitions, there is no restriction on participation; anyone can compete. This arena includes games that are sponsored by different countries, such as the U.S. Open, Mexico Open, European Open, and Korean Open.

Combined sports games include the Summer Olympic Games, Summer World University Games, World Games, Pan American Games, Central American and Caribbean Sports Games, All Africa Games, Asian Games, and Goodwill Games.

The competitive aspect of taekwondo, the matches in which athletes pit their power and skill against each other, is the highlight of the sport. The purpose of competition is to provide an arena in which athletes can measure their skills against those of other athletes. A match is conducted within a limited time and is judged within specific parameters. A judge reviews the legal attack points, the power and displacement of punches, and the striking positions of the feet, all within limited rules. The perfection of taekwondo skills can be realized in the spirit of fair play and within a safe environment.

RULES OF COMPETITION

Taekwondo match rules are action-limiting regulations that became official. Today taekwondo competition is structured in such a way that only certain skills are regarded as legitimate scoring actions. Athletes must perform their skills safely and exceptionally. To do so, they must master the skills for the competitive arena and thoroughly understand the rules of the match.

In taekwondo, there are skills related to the feet *(tae)* and skills related to the hands *(kwon)*. Foot skills include any skill executed by the foot, below the ankle only. Any strike with any other part of the leg or with the knee is restricted. Hand skills are performed with a tight fist. Punching by means of the index and middle fingers of the fist is permitted to the torso only, regardless of angle or position of strike. Unlike kickboxing, punches to the face are not permitted; only the feet may be used to strike the face. Taekwondo has evolved to allow punching with the knuckles pointed up, to the outside, or down. However, uppercut punches are not permitted.

During the match, any attack below the waist is restricted. Hits with the hands to any part of the body above the waist except for the face, back of the head, and spine are permitted. Attacks that involve pulling, grabbing, wrestling, or holding are restricted. Prohibited acts include crossing the boundary line; evading by turning the back to the opponent; intentionally falling down; avoiding the match; grabbing, holding, or pushing the opponent; attacking below the waist; pretending injury; butting or attacking with the knee; hitting an opponent's face with the hand; and uttering undesirable remarks. Any misconduct on the part of a contestant or coach is also prohibited. These acts are penalized with a kyoung-go, or warning penalty, and cost half of a point.

Because direct contact is permitted, protective arm, instep, foot, shin, torso, groin, and head gear is mandatory. Points are only given for attacks to the trunk protector, excluding the spine and back of the head.

Points are awarded based on the judge's evaluation of the skill with focus on the displacement of the person being hit. One point is earned for an attack to the trunk protector, 2 points are earned for an attack to the head, and 1 additional point is earned if the opponent is knocked down or really rocked off balance (referred to as *standing down*) and the referee counts. Legal scoring areas include the midsection of the trunk (the part covered by the trunk protector) and the face and head, including both ears.

In addition to warning penalties, a more severe penalty, gam-jeom, costs a contestant 1 point for the following actions: attacking the opponent after kal-yeo, or break, is called; attacking a fallen opponent; throwing down the opponent by grabbing the opponent's attacking foot in the air with the arm or by pushing the opponent with the hand; intentionally attacking the opponent's face with the hand; or interrupting the progress of the match (contestant or coach). Clearly, fair play is strictly enforced.

Because use of the hands and feet is restricted, it is essential for a fighter to develop the skills of the feet. Attacks that involve grabbing the head or hitting or butting the face of an opponent, or attacking the legs in a wrestling fashion so that the opponent is unbalanced, are restricted. Athletes must rely on skill alone. The power of the strike is not restricted; direct hitting is permitted as long as athletes are in the mandatory protective gear. Striking power, which is allowed in the match, cannot be properly evaluated in other events such as poomse or yaksok gyorugi; therein lies the importance of the rules for direct hitting in competitive sparring.

1

Finding Motivation and Setting Goals

Training and motivational goals vary depending on the trainee's age, gender, circumstances, and environment. Trainees pursue their own path for satisfying their desire to transform resolve into action. Through the physical activity of taekwondo, trainees begin to aspire to a higher level of achievement and skill.

Motivation for training can be internal or external. This motivation leads athletes in the direction of the goals they deem most important. In general, trainees begin with external motivation and eventually develop internal motivation through achievement and a growing interest in the sport.

External motivation comes from a source outside the trainee. A trainee might wish to emulate an outstanding athlete or an admired movie hero or heroine. The support and encouragement of family members or friends may lead a person to pursue taekwondo. Sometimes social or economic situations motivate self-improvement. Or, the trainee may simply be interested in sport and exercise.

Internal motivation, on the other hand, is the trainee's inner desire. It might involve the desire to achieve mental discipline through physical exercise or to pursue beauty through physical movement. Some trainees might wish to improve their health and physical strength or manage their weight. Others might participate in taekwondo to develop self-defense skills.

Good instructors motivate their students by creating a sense of trust. Instructors achieve this trust by setting good examples, establishing effective and systematic exercise plans, providing diverse projects including demonstration and breaking, using audiovisual tools for training, and reviewing matches with students.

Competitors who decide to try the sparring ring do so in exploration. If they are not eager to fight, then curiosity to test skills against another, to test oneself, or just to check it out may be the driving force. This path of exploration can take many roads. On that road of discovery the fighting spirit is nurtured through achievement and fine-tuned with skill. Defeat could strengthen the appetite for improvement or deflate the drive to move forward. Competitive fighters use wins and losses for long-term growth. They have a strong desire to win. Whether this desire comes from nature or is the result of nurturing doesn't really matter. It's what is done with that spirit that shapes the fighter.

SETTING GOALS

Goals help maintain motivation. Goal setting creates a plan for the future backed by the desire to do something concrete. Goals should be explicit to allow a trainee to recognize the challenges of the task and provide a time line for achievement.

A trainee who doesn't set goals lacks direction and can have little hope for future success. This trainee's desire has no focus. Physical performance will be diminished because the trainee lacks direction. Achievement and positive feedback provide the fuel for elite fighters.

Those individuals training at higher levels, such as black belt or potential Olympic athletes, should set proper goals and strive to achieve those goals by performing tasks with an enthusiastic attitude. Goal setting and achievement provide momentum to the training process and create pleasure and satisfaction through the sharing of a common activity with other trainees. The sense of self-accomplishment obtained through goal achievement greatly improves mental focus and physical performance.

Through goal setting, the trainee knows what to do and how to do it. After developing goals, trainees can concentrate on the tasks required to achieve those goals. A positive attitude enables mental concentration and physical persistence in an effort to achieve the goals regardless of changing circumstances.

To build stamina for training and improving performance, trainees should have a clear understanding of what they want to achieve. Taekwondo goals should center on improving physical health, mastering skills, achieving performance benchmarks, and developing a competitive attitude. For improving physical health, trainees may set goals to improve basic physical strength; increase flexibility, reaction speed, and agility; or control weight.

For mastering skills, goals may include learning basic posture and kicking skills; developing new skills such as those demanded at belt screenings; learning skills related to match strategy such as attacking skills, striking back,

Elite fighters train with competitive goals in mind. Reaching goals improves focus and confidence, which means more success on the mat.

kicking by spinning, jump kicking, and back kicking; or understanding games rules for the license of skill required.

Developing a competitive mentality also requires goals. A trainee develops confidence through sufficient practice. Goals for achieving performance benchmarks focus on performance in matches. For example, a trainee might desire to improve her match skill by engaging in sufficient exercise. Through drills and training, she learns skills for attack and defense, develops the ability to estimate attacks by opponents, and increases her reaction speed. Participation in local and goodwill games is an excellent way to refine strategy and reaction times. Any opportunity to simulate the circumstances of a match adds to the athlete's experience, which in turn diminishes anxiety, controls excitement, builds confidence, increases the ability to read opponents, and expands on the variety of situations that may be encountered. Training in a gym is no match for experience in the ring.

Goals need to be challenging but realistic. Goals that can be achieved without much effort reduce the sense of accomplishment. Unrealistic goals reduce the likelihood of achievement and may discourage trainees. By setting realistic goals, trainees can reach a higher level of skill even if the goal is a bit difficult to achieve. Successful goal achievement improves the chances of continued involvement and increases satisfaction.

Long-term goals are important for defining a vision and direction for the future. Short-term goals provide feedback for realizing long-term goals and also help maintain motivation. As taekwondo athletes improve their skill through physical exercise and training, they persist in achieving long-term goals as their level of performance rises.

Short-term goals should be obtainable within three months. Good short-term goals might include mastering certain techniques such as kicks or attack tactics. Preparing for the test for rank advancement can be a short-term goal, but the test should be scheduled for a month when no match is scheduled, if possible. Also, trainees should look to improve basics such as flexibility, reaction speed, agility, persistence, and weight control.

Intermediate goals take four to six months to achieve. A test for rank advancement or participation in an upcoming competition might be an intermediate goal.

Long-term goals require one to three years to achieve. Long-range competitions or a screening for a black belt would be considered long-term goals. Advanced athletes might desire to become national team members or to join their country's Olympic team.

The advanced athlete will strive to harmonize all aspects of the training regimen. Mental attitude plays an important part in the foundation of an elite fighter. A certain fearlessness is embodied in the competitive spirit and gives spark to the confidence to win. The athlete's psyche must also be prepared to overcome hurdles of defeat, injury, or unfairness in order to move forward in the competitive arena (see chapter 8).

According to your individual goals, outline a schedule for each day, week, and month. The daily timetable becomes the basis for monthly training. Record daily drills in detail and note what you experienced during training. Which drills were insufficient? Which were successful? You will be able to use your training notes to set more precise goals, leading to skill improvement and increased confidence.

OVERCOMING FATIGUE AND TEMPORARY SLUMPS

Fatigue can result from the physical and mental stresses of daily life. Long-term training doesn't exempt one from the effects of fatigue or the energy drain caused by fear of competition. Fatigue reduces concentration and performance and increases the risk of injury. Athletes should work with the coach or instructor to evaluate whether their fatigue is due to lack of rest or to repetition and boredom in the training plan. Fatigue is a warning sign that should not be ignored. Without proper attention, a fatigued athlete could decline even further into a slump.

I am reminded of a time when I was coaching the U.S. team in an international competition. One of the team members had made the cut to the semifinals. This athlete had excellent technique and a good chance to win. However, in order to reach the semifinals he had participated in several elimination matches, and he was showing signs of fatigue. During the semi-final match, the athlete had many opportunities to attack. As coach, I yelled instructions from the sidelines that fell on deaf ears. Ultimately he lost. The athlete heard me perfectly well, but his body had no more to give. He was so exhausted that his excellent technique was useless. Upon further inquiry, I found that the athlete knew beforehand that his opponent was a gold medalist in another international competition. This psychological arrow helped to expel any winning attitude that might have carried him past the fatigue.

The point is that fatigue is an important training component that must be addressed. Maintaining skill training under mild fatigue may improve the athlete's physical condition for the next match. Muscle fatigue is experienced during a match, so practicing under this condition helps athletes prepare for competition. Therefore, much attention should be given to physical conditioning, including muscular and cardiovascular endurance.

A temporary stall, or plateau, is a stagnation or decline in skill improvement. This feeling of going nowhere often occurs in beginning and even intermediate students. After a rapid influx of new material and techniques, boredom sets in as these techniques are practiced over and over. It is important to vary the training schedule by using different methods, such as the partial versus whole and concentration versus allocation methods (see chapter 2). This will help spread the training focus, generate motivation, and keep things mentally interesting. Understanding the reasons for particular moves and how they apply in the ring or in self-defense also generates motivation to achieve goals.

Veteran athletes are not immune to periods of disinterest or little improvement. View this time as preparation for greater skill improvement in the next stage. Understanding what plateaus are and how to approach them helps alleviate the fear that training has come to a full stop. Stay rested and consult the instructor to mix up the training plan. Take this time to dig deeper in the sport, its history, and its evolution. Foster a sense of confidence and new interest in training to overcome these temporary lapses.

In general, slumps appear in the latter half of the training sequence. During a slump, the athlete experiences a sense of taking two steps back and one step forward. A slump may be the result of psychological factors such as emotional tension, overtraining, disappointment in physical ability, time away from the sport due to injury, discouragement with referee calls, or a losing streak despite sufficient training.

Slumps are very real and can happen to the best of athletes. I, for one, suffered an injury that required a three-month recovery. It was a significant challenge to stay on course and battle the despondency that set in. I spent many hours rethinking my career as an athlete and my life goals. Luckily I had plenty of support and encouragement to make me believe I could fight again. During the recovery period, I watched tapes of other matches and began to visualize myself back in the ring, even raising my personal benchmark for achievement. I knew that I had a good foundation of ability and that it was the mental game I had to play.

Learn to recognize a slump and overcome it wisely. Choose the proper practice method (see chapter 2) and structure training so that it fits the environment. If skills stagnate, continuous training will only increase tedium and fatigue and cause a loss of interest. The problem must be diagnosed and training must be improved to rekindle interest and build confidence. Discover new motivation and revisit goals for possible adjustment.

2

Training to Win

Taekwondo skill is a byproduct of smart practice. Large amounts of repetitive practice alone do not guarantee skill improvement. Skill improvement may result from mindless repetitive practice, but bad habits may also form, ultimately interfering with skill improvement. In addition, trainees may lose interest in practice drills and face a temporary stagnation in improvement. For the casual athlete, such stagnation may not be a problem. However, for the competitive athlete, training apathy must be resolved if there is to be future growth.

Persistent training helps to reduce the mental tension athletes feel when they finally stand before an opponent in a match. In taekwondo, an athlete is expected to adapt to the opponent's strategy and to the changing tactics of the match. Winning or losing in taekwondo is a product of the ability to use basic physical strength, to use match strategies, to control emotions, and to use skills to control a match.

Practice conditions influence a trainee's opportunities for skill improvement. Complex factors such as age, personality, physical strength, technical level, experience, motivation, and environment also play a part. An instructor's training methods and the trainee's acceptance of those methods also have great bearing on the ability of the trainee to improve both skill and competitive ability.

Challenging goals and high motivation fuel effective practice. An effective practice plan is tailored to the needs of the individual.

As in all sports, students learn in stages. Motor skills are acquired through visual cues, processing movement with knowledge. A particular technique does not become automatic when first presented. A trainee goes through three stages to acquire skills:

1. Beginner. At this time the student has some visual understanding of the movement and adopts the information.
2. Intermediate. The student processes the visual information and begins to connect the muscle sensations with each technique.
3. Advanced. Proficiency is achieved through repetitive practice such that visual cues, knowledge of the technique, and muscle memory coordinate to effect an automatic action.

Beginners learn through simple explanations and demonstrations of basic postures and skills. Techniques are broken down into singular motions that are easy to understand and perform. This method of teaching partial components helps to build confidence and motivates the student to greater learning. (See Partial Practice on page 11.)

During the intermediate stage, knowledge of techniques and the resulting muscle sensations of the techniques are united, even if imperfectly. A training method that introduces more complex skills helps to reduce boredom and generate interest at this level. It is also beneficial to keep the training varied enough such that trainees have adequate information and time to correct posture and movement. (See Allocation Practice on page 10.)

The advanced stage emerges when trainees can practice independently and accurately. It is at this stage that competitive skill and abilities can be improved through repetitive practice of basic postures and motions. The trainee not only improves skill but also begins to incorporate the elements of speed and accuracy. Combining skill with experience in the ring allows the athlete to learn visual cues indicating the direction, speed, and ability of an opponent and to adjust appropriately. The ultimate goal is to produce quick and precise reactions that do not require conscious thought for the actions to occur. (See Concentration Practice and Whole Practice on pages 10 and 11.)

The formula for power is mass times speed $(P = m \times s)$. Power equals the quantity of matter multiplied by the speed of delivery. In other words, strong kicking means fast kicking. In taekwondo, speed can be improved as follows:

- Delivering a front-leg kick from an upright back stance produces better speed than delivering the same kick from a centered low stance.
- Delivering a kick from a stance in which body weight shifts over the front leg is faster than when the weight is over the rear leg.
- Moving the entire body forward for a punch or kick increases the amount of motion, thus increasing speed.

- A forward kick (snap kick, high kick, axe kick, pushing kick) is quicker than a rear or rotation kick (round kick, back kick, hook kick). The torso faces forward and does not turn.
- A combination kick in which the direction is in a single line, such as a round kick with spin back or a round kick with a hook kick, is quick.
- Speed may be increased by increasing flexibility through breath control or yelling a gi-hap, which relaxes the body and reduces inner resistance.

Effective training develops a fighter who reacts automatically with accuracy, power, and speed.

GUIDELINES FOR EFFECTIVE PRACTICE

Sport taekwondo consists of specific motions and skills. Practice methods are quite complex, composed of poomse (forms), defense techniques (striking, kicking), and sparring.

Effective practice is tailored to the abilities, physical strengths, and motivation of the individual trainee. It is important to apportion the length of practice time among the many taekwondo skills.

Concentration and Allocation Practice Methods

In the concentration method of practice, one skill is practiced over a certain period of time with few or no rest periods. The allocation method, on the other hand, incorporates intermittent rests and it reviews more than one skill. The allocation method is effective when working over a longer period of time, such as a whole day or week. The concentration method might be used for a single session of practice.

Concentration Practice

The concentration method of practice is effective for training movements in a short period (20 to 30 minutes) with little or no rest. This method is good for correcting the inaccurate movements of beginners because it breaks down the technique into segments and focuses on one segment at a time (partial practice). Partial practice also builds confidence, generates interest in new and more complex tasks, and brings about routine movements.

For the competitive athlete, the concentration method is beneficial when there is a short period of time before an event and a particular technique needs to be perfected. For example, in certain match situations athletes need to use visualization to develop attack or counterattack strategies. Then the athletes can repeatedly practice the circumstance to the point of automation. For example, an athlete may want to practice countering a rear-leg round kick, rear-leg axe kick, or spin back kick. The counterstrategy might be to either round kick from the same spot, shuffle back, and kick at the same time, or to shuffle to the side and kick at the same time. In any case, the focus should be on that particular circumstance. The athlete should practice until the counterattack becomes comfortable, quick, and automatic.

Allocation Practice

When more time is available, allocating practice time to certain skills might be a better training method. For example, the athlete could execute a specific kick for 10 minutes with a 5-minute rest. Repeating this 15-minute segment four times generates an hour of practice. This method can be used when there is a need to continuously practice one skill, when practicing one skill is needed to make the actions automatic, or when it is necessary to correct bad habits. Another approach might be to practice one kick for 10 minutes and rest for 5 minutes, practice a different kick for 10 minutes and rest for 5, practice a third kick for 10 minutes and rest for 5, and practice a fourth kick for 10 minutes and then rest.

Another approach is to incorporate secondary skills into the rest periods. For example, stretch for 10 minutes and then practice steps for 5, practice new kicks or combinations for 10 minutes and a shuffle step for 5, and then practice step sparring for 10 minutes and run in place for 5. The goal is to mix up the training so that it includes many elements. This method requires high levels of energy.

Finally, the allocation of skills can be broken down into a weekly schedule. For example, the first segment of every day might be dedicated to kicks, the next segment to steps, the next segment to endurance exercises, and so on.

The allocation method allows the competitive athlete to refresh different skills and it reduces boredom. Sometimes changing the rhythm of practice refreshes the material. An analogy might be made with music: The concentration method could be likened to listening to one song over and over until the listener has memorized the lyrics and music, whereas the allocation method allows the listener to experience songs in different disciplines (jazz, rock, classical) so as to have more exposure to music as a whole.

Partial and Whole Practice Methods

Deciding which of these two practice methods to use depends on which method will be more effective in achieving the practice goal: practicing the entire task repeatedly as a unit (whole practice) or dividing the task into several parts (partial practice).

Taekwondo skill is a complex structure built of basic movements. Beginners are introduced to overall movements via demonstration and then partial movements are taught. When partial movements become familiar, parts can be combined one at a time until the entire unit is integrated. The unit is then practiced until the beginner can competently perform the movement as a whole.

Partial Practice

In the partial practice method, trainees are taught individual components of skills. This method is best for beginners. However, even seasoned athletes can use this method in order to glean the most efficiency in a particular technique. In preparation for a match an athlete may want to break a strategic move into parts and practice each part independently. For example, a fake, step, and then double round spin back combination would be broken down into three or four segments. For partial practice the athlete might practice just the fake, making sure the whole body exhibits a perceived motion. Then the athlete might work on the step in connection with the fake for quickness and distance control. Third, practicing the double round kick as a segment helps to prepare the athlete for the combined motion. Finally, the athlete works in the spin back kick as a separate item or links it to the double round kick. Mastering a particular skill will help the athlete to feel more comfortable by reducing anxiety and confusion.

Whole Practice

The whole method is best for practicing poomse, combination kicks, or multiple step and kick strategies. In this method, trainees repeatedly practice one unit. Athletes should have good physical conditioning and an understanding of circumstances in which techniques are used. In the partial method, one combination, such as the fake, step, and double round spin back combination, is used to demonstrate how a technique can be broken down. In the whole method, this combination is practiced in its entirety. For the competitive athlete, whole practice turns complex movements into smooth, rhythmic reactions to particular match circumstances. That is why it is imperative for competitive fighters to gain experience in the ring and then bring those circumstances back to the dojang for analysis and improvement.

Speed and Precision

Speed and precision should be included in a trainee's goals, though the emphasis may change depending on the technique being performed. For example, let's say an athlete needs to practice the counterattack to a rear round kick and clinch. If the counter is a punch and a jump spin back kick, then accuracy might be the focus. On the other hand, speed would be imperative if the counterattack is a fast round kick, shuffle back, and jump spin back.

Speed and accuracy are closely related in sports that require both elements. To be accurate in performing skill, it is necessary to reduce speed. Conversely, to perform a skill with speed, it is necessary to reduce accuracy. It is important to focus on one aspect, speed or accuracy, according to the circumstance being practiced. Over time, gradually incorporate the other element.

A referee's perception of a score could be broken down into 70 percent accuracy and 30 percent impact or power (weight multiplied by speed). Often a strike isn't right on target but the power of the strike overrides a slight inaccuracy. With speed, an athlete can make accurate contact before the opponent has time to react. Speed also creates confusion for opponents. If they are not fast enough, they may not be able to react in time. Accuracy and power without speed will not contribute to a winning edge.

TRAINING PLAN

An athlete's goals provide direction for improving and maintaining match performance. The highest level of skill improvement is possible when psychological and physical aspects of training compliment each other and are in harmony with the improvement of match skill.

Training to improve match skill includes physical strength training, basic skill training, tactical training, and mental training. Effective training reinforces a strong mentality and desire to win. It also fosters the ability to cope with change.

Before planning a training schedule for a particular match, gather information about the event such as environment and climate, number of athletes attending the event, and time available for training before the event. By tailoring the training schedule to the event, it is possible to adjust and improve skills based on event factors.

During the training period, all of the athlete's energy is concentrated on preparing for the contest. Emphasize physical strength, basic skills, endurance, power, agility, flexibility, and tactics. Sparring training should also take place.

Whether an athlete trains once or twice a day depends on the athlete's condition and rhythm. If training takes place at an all-day camp, training should be scheduled three times a day. Long-distance running, uphill running, stair training, and short sprints should be included in the training plan. If prior knowledge of a match dictates special training, a plan should be tailored to the athlete and the skills needed for that particular match.

Schedule a winding-up period during the week or two before the match. Adjust conditioning and improve speed through stretching and light kicks. During this time, strengthen psychological preparation through mental training. Psychological preparation is a crucial element of this period.

A recuperation period of one to two weeks should follow a match. During this period, treat injuries and continue psychological training in preparation for the next match. Also during this period, evaluate the strong and weak points of the previous match and begin preparation for the next event.

The training plan can be divided into yearly, monthly, weekly, and daily plans. A yearly plan should be established from the perspective of long-term training and should take into consideration extremely hot and cold periods, vacation time, and the need for rest before and after matches. The monthly plan consists of a natural repetition of four weeks and should be based on the weekly plan. Table 2.1 is an example of a weekly training plan. Games usually take place during weekends, so the training plan should maintain a sense of rhythm throughout the month. The daily plan is the basis for the weekly and monthly plans. When the daily plan is followed faithfully, the weekly and monthly plans will proceed smoothly.

The daily plan takes into account the skill level of the athlete. Time for exercise, types of training, training and exercise intensity, and number of repetitions are part of the plan. The daily training plan is divided into five stages:

1. Purpose and motivation: Without direction or goals, training is meaningless. You must know what to strive for in the exercise plan.

2. Preparatory exercise: Include stretching and special training for reinforcing physical strength.

3. Main exercise: Plan this stage in detail. For example, will you develop basic skills; learn new skills; focus on skills for scoring such as the round kick, axe kick, and back kick; or engage in tactics training? Should skills be organized from easy to difficult? Should each practice concentrate on one skill or should each practice be divided among many skills? Should the emphasis be on speed or on precision? Be sure to include mental training.

4. Winding-down exercise: Include a period of cool-down and stretching to relax muscles and return the heart rate to normal.

Table 2.1   Weekly Training Schedule

Day	Type of training	Specific actions
Monday	Physical conditioning	
	Muscular endurance	Jump rope—10 min
	Muscular strength	Push-ups, sit-ups, leg lifts, rabbit jumps in place—2 min
	Flexibility	Stretching—10 min
	Agility	Side steps—1 min; running in place—1 min
	Power	Maximum running, 50 to 100 m (55 to 109 yd)—3 min; jump knees to chest—1 min
	Speed	Resistance running in place—2 to 3 min
	Basic kicks and steps	Snap kicks through punching
	Running forward kicks	Combination basic and step kicks
	Running sparring	Run to end of gym and back; train for automatic responses to certain attacks or counterattacks
	Paddle kicks	Scoring kicks, mainly round kicks and punching (scoring area)
Tuesday	Physical conditioning	
	Muscular endurance	Run cross country 3 to 4 mi (5 to 6 km)—30 min
	Muscular strength	Standing elbow knee touches, 2 sets—5 to 10 min; duck walk—2 min
	Flexibility	Stretching—10 min
	Agility	Jump knees to chest 20 to 30 times; fast running 20 to 30 m (22 to 33 yd)—3 min; short-distance relay running—3 min
	Power	Maximum running, 50 to 100 m (55 to 109 yd)—3 min; jump knees to chest—1 min
	Speed	Resistance running in place—2 to 3 min
	Basic kicks and steps	Snap kicks through punching
	Knee and step sparring	Knee kicks with steps
	Paddle kicks	Round kicks with punching; clinching with punching; cut kicks with punching
	Paddle circuit kicks	Basic kicks with partner (1:1) or paddle kicks (3:1)
	Paddle sparring	Two paddles (1:1), using various target positions for kicks and punches
Wednesday	Physical conditioning	
	Muscular endurance	Jump rope—10 min; interval training—10 min
	Muscular strength	Push-ups, sit-ups, leg lifts, rabbit jumps in place—2 min
	Flexibility	Stretching—10 min
	Agility	Side steps—1 min; jumps with leg split—1 min
	Power	Maximum running, 50 to 100 m (55 to 109 yd)—3 min; partner jumps—2 to 3 min; jump knees to chest—1 min
	Speed	Resistance running in place—2 to 3 min
	Basic kicks and steps	Snap kicks through punching
	Running forward kicks	Combination basic and step kicks
	Running sparring	Run to end of gym and back; train for automatic responses to certain attacks or counterattacks
	Paddle kicks	Scoring kicks, mainly round kicks and punching (scoring area)

Day	Type of training	Specific actions
Thursday	Physical conditioning	
	Muscular endurance	Run cross country 3 to 4 mi (5 to 6 km)—30 min
	Muscular strength	Standing elbow-knee touches, 2 sets—5 to 10 min; duck walk—2 min
	Flexibility	Stretching—5 to 10 min; directional leg lifts—5 min
	Agility	Jump knees to chest, 20 to 30 times; maximum running, 20 to 30 m (22 to 33 yd)—3 min; short-distance relay running—1 min
	Power	Maximum running, 50 m (55 yd)—3 min; jump knees to chest—1 min
	Speed	Uphill and maximum running—5 to 10 min
	Basic kicks and steps	Snap kicks through punching
	Knee and step sparring	Knee kicks with steps
	Paddle kicks	Round kicks with punching; clinching with punching; cut kicks with punching
	Paddle circuit kicks	Paddle kicks (3:1)
	Paddle sparring	Two paddles (1:1), using various target positions for kicks and punches
Friday	Physical conditioning	
	Muscular endurance	Paddle circuit training with partners (3:1)
	Muscular strength	Push-ups, sit-ups, leg lifts, rabbit jumps in place—2 min
	Flexibility	Stretching—10 min
	Agility	Side steps—1 min; running in place—1 min
	Power	Maximum running, 50 to 100 m (55 to 109 yd)—3 min; frog long jump—2 min
	Speed	Resistance running—2 to 3 min; speed kicks with partner or bag, 5 sets—5 min
	Basic kicks and steps	Snap kicks through punching
	Running forward kicks	Combination basic and step kicks
	Running sparring	Run to end of gym and back; train for automatic responses to certain attacks or counterattacks
	Paddle kicks	Scoring kicks, mainly round kicks and punching (scoring area)
	Kick-bag sparring	Kicks and punches in response to imaginary attacks and counterattacks
Saturday	Physical conditioning	
	Muscular endurance	Jump rope—10 min; run stairs—5 min
	Muscular strength	Push-ups, sit-ups, leg lifts, rabbit jumps in place—2 min
	Flexibility	Stretching—10 min
	Agility	Side steps—1 min; running in place—1 min
	Power	Frog long jump—2 min
	Speed	Resistance running—2 to 3 min
	Basic kicks and steps	Snap kicks through punching
	Advanced kicks	Special skills; advanced kicks
	Chest-pad training	Impact noise drill; cutting or pushing kicks; scoring kicks, mainly round kicks and punching (scoring area)
	Chest-pad sparring	Attacks and counterattacks with partner, mimicking competitive situations
	Free sparring	With partner (1:1) or two partners (2:1) for three 2-min rounds

5. Evaluation: The evaluation phase completes the plan. During training, have an instructor analyze strong and weak areas. Use the strong points as motivation for achieving goals. Evaluate deficiencies and discover ways to improve those areas.

The training period includes activities to improve physical conditioning, such as weight training, circuit training, interval training, and cross country running. Basic attacks and counterattacks are included so that athletes can maintain their skill in these basic techniques. When training basic attacks, attack with steps using the front foot and include turning kicks. When training basic counterattacks, attack with cutting or pushing kicks (including the punch), with steps and feints, and with side steps.

The training period also includes more advanced training. Kicks include running kicks, combination kicks (feints, steps, and punches), jumping kicks, turn kicks, counterkicks, running sparring, and step sparring. For paddle kicks, the holder determines the direction and presentation of the paddle. Surprise presentation of the paddle helps to develop the athlete's reaction time and target accuracy. In kick-bag training, combine attack and counterattack kicks, with and without steps (include side steps, jumping kicks, and punches). Kick-bag training also develops power. Free sparring and mental training round out training. Be sure to cover any new rules as well, as rules may change, and prepare for changes in scoring strategies and tactics.

WARMING UP AND STRETCHING

Taekwondo sparring requires flexible actions of the joints that may not be typical movements. An agile athlete can execute taekwondo attacks and counterattacks at a higher level of skill because the muscles and joints move smoothly. This flexibility, connected with explosive power, is vital for success in the ring. Be mindful of going beyond gentle resistance because muscle damage could result. As with aerobic conditioning, flexibility needs to be developed gradually to avoid injury.

Stretching raises body temperature before exercise, increasing the effectiveness of a workout while helping to protect against muscle injury. It is also important to stretch after exercise, when the muscles and joints are loose, in order to improve flexibility.

Before stretching, a preparatory aerobic exercise such as jumping rope should be performed. After the preparatory exercise, relax the muscles with stretching and then move on to the main practice. The main practice should begin at a simple level and progress to more strenuous drills. Using a gradational scale of exertion will help to prevent injury. After finishing the main practice, cool down and stretch in order to return major muscle groups to a resting state.

The time allocated for stretching depends on the environment. In a warm environment, 10 to 20 minutes of stretching is desirable. In a cooler environment, stretching should be performed until a slight sweat is broken. It is necessary to relax the muscles before a match by stretching for 30 to 40 minutes. After that time, maintain body temperature and sustain muscle flexibility by wearing sweats or other warm clothes.

When stretching is done regularly outside of the dojang, for example while watching television, muscle relaxation can be speeded up and the effect of the main practice may be increased. In a long-term plan, continuous stretching and effective weight training will increase muscular power.

Warm-Up Exercises

Warm-up exercises increase body temperature and help relax the muscles and joints before practice or stretches. Take 10 to 15 minutes to warm up before stretching. In some dojangs the instructor will lead the warm-up and stretching. However, it is prudent for the athlete to warm up and stretch before class in case there isn't time to cover all aspects of a good warm-up. At least 15 to 30 seconds should be allowed for each warm-up activity. Following are some suggested activities.

Begin by engaging in mild aerobic activity such as jumping rope or performing jumping jacks. Follow with standing elbow–knee touches with bouncing. Stand with feet shoulder-width apart. Jump slightly and lift your right knee, touching it with your left elbow. Return to the starting position and then lift your left knee, touching it with your right elbow.

After the standing elbow–knee touches, move into neck rotations. Stand with feet shoulder-width apart. Rotate your head to the front, right side, back, and left side. Then reverse the rotation and rotate to the left.

After the neck rotation, perform shoulder rotations. Stand with feet shoulder-width apart. Begin by rolling your shoulders to the front. Then reverse the direction and roll the shoulders back. Don't move your elbows out from your body, and be sure to tense the muscles in the shoulders and neck.

Hip rotations follow the shoulder rotations. Rotate the hips left, back, and right and return to the starting position. Reverse the direction, rotating the hips right, back, left, and then to the starting position.

Move on to knee and leg exercises, beginning with squats. Stand with feet shoulder-width apart, hands on knees. Squat toward the floor, keeping your hands on your knees. Stand up. After squats, perform knee rotations, alternating right and left. Stand with feet shoulder-width apart, knees slightly bent, and hands on knees. Rotate knees to the left, then forward, and then to the right.

After the knee rotations, half-windmill the body. Stand with feet more than shoulder-width apart. Bring the right hand to the left foot as you extend the left hand upward, eyes watching your left hand. Go the other direction, bringing your left hand to your right foot as you watch your right hand extend upward.

For upper-body rotation, stand with feet shoulder-width apart. Bend at the waist, lowering hands to the floor. Rotate to the left. Lean to the left side and slightly backward, bringing hands around. Stretch hands upward and back, rotating to the right and returning to the starting position. Reverse direction and circle from right to left.

Follow the upper-body rotation with punches while running in place. As you bring your left knee up, punch with your right hand. As you lift your right knee, punch with your left hand.

Move on to the waist twist. Stand with feet shoulder-width apart, arms in mountain block position (arms out to sides, elbows perpendicular to body, and forearms straight up). Twist at the waist to the right and then twist to the left. Return to the starting position.

Finish the warm-up with eyeball rotations. Look down with both eyes, then to the right, then to the left, then upward.

Stretching Exercises

Plan on spending 30 to 60 seconds stretching each part of the body (neck, eyes, shoulders, elbows, wrists, waist, hips, calves, hamstrings, thighs, ankles, and feet). Use good sense when stretching if an injury prohibits certain exercises. In some dojangs the instructor will lead the warm-up and stretching. However, as mentioned previously, it is prudent to warm up and stretch before class in case there isn't time to cover all aspects of a good warm-up.

After warming up, you are ready for stretching. Begin with shoulder stretches. Raise your left arm and bend it behind your head, reaching for the back of your right shoulder. Grab your left elbow with your right hand and pull gently. Switch arms. Next clasp your hands behind your back and lift your arms as you bend forward at the waist.

After stretching the shoulders, move on to side stretches. Stand with your hands on your hips. Lift your left hand and lean to the right, reaching over your head. Switch directions, lifting your right hand and leaning to the left. Now stand and bend forward, touching the floor. This will stretch your lower back, hips, and hamstrings. Stand again and place your hands on your hips. Lean back at the waist.

You are now ready to stretch the legs. Begin with a standing, short-spread calf stretch. Stand with your right knee slightly bent and your left leg extended to the side. Gently lift the toes of your left foot. Squat into a low, long-spread leg stretch. Slowly squat all the way to the floor while stretching one leg to the side. Shift your body weight forward for balance.

Sit on the floor and perform a butterfly stretch. Bring the soles of your feet together. Grab your toes and lean forward about 45 degrees. To decrease pressure on the lower back, you can move your feet farther from your groin, or you can bring your heels close to your groin, place your hands on the floor behind your back, and straighten your spine.

While on the floor, perform the seated spinal twist for the waist. Extend your left leg. Bend your right knee and place your right foot on the opposite side of your left knee. Place your left elbow behind your right knee and twist to the right. Bring your right arm behind your back to facilitate the twist and support yourself. Switch legs and direction.

After the spinal twist, perform the ankle twist. Hold your foot and rotate your ankle in one direction and then in the other direction. Switch feet.

Remain on the floor for the hurdler's stretch. Stretch out your left leg. Bend your right knee and turn out your foot. Place your foot against the inside of your left leg. Reach for the toes of your left leg, leaning at the waist toward the outstretched leg. Repeat with the other leg.

Move into the side-kick stretch. Bend your right knee and bring your right foot toward your groin. Stretch out your left leg to the side. Lean toward your left leg and grab your foot. Switch legs.

Still on the floor, split your legs apart. Lift your arms overhead and stretch to the left. Return to the starting position and lean to the right. Now reach forward with both arms, bending at the waist. Attempt to touch the floor with your face or, if you are less flexible, with your elbows. This stretch can also be done from a standing position. To enhance this exercise, extend the stretch out on your heels as in a middle split. Bend forward and use your hands on the floor for support. Then turn the torso, split left, and hold the position for 15 seconds, and then reverse to a split right position and hold. Slowly return to a standing position and shake out the legs.

Next it's time to stretch the lower back, abdomen, and hips. Lie on your back. Lift your left leg, keeping the leg straight, until it is at a 90-degree angle with your upper body. Twist at the waist and hip and lower your left leg across your body to the right side. Hold your arms out to each side to keep your upper body flat on the floor. Return to the starting position and repeat with the right leg.

The next stretch can be done while sitting on the floor or while lying on your back. It stretches and relaxes the lower back and hips. Bring the knees up to the chest. Lower the knees to the left, lift them back to the chest, and then lower them to the right. To enhance this exercise, extend the arms at right angles to the body, arms flat on the floor. Raise your legs in a straight position and slowly lower them together to the left, using your arms for stability. Then slowly raise the legs straight up and lower them to the right. Repeat two or three times.

Still lying on your back, lift your legs. Move your feet in a cycling motion, first cycling forward and then cycling backward.

If you are extremely flexible and are comfortable bending backward, you may want to try a back-bend stretch. While lying on your back, place your hands on the floor next to your head. Push yourself up into a back bend, lifting your abdomen toward the ceiling and arching your back off the floor.

Lie on your abdomen again for a final stretch of the lower back and chest. Arch your back, lifting your head and chest off the floor. Slightly twist your upper body and look to the left. Gently twist the other way and look to the right. If your lower back is tender, injured, or restricted, bring one knee forward with the other leg outstretched. Raise your torso up on your arms and drop the hip of the outstretched leg to the floor. Hold the stretch for a few seconds and switch legs.

For the final stretch, do a running ready-stance stretch. In this stretch, you will look like a hurdler in the running blocks, waiting for the starting gun. Stand and step forward with one foot. Bend the front knee and straighten the rear leg. The front foot remains flat on the floor, but the toes of the back foot are bent.

INJURY PREVENTION AND TREATMENT

Those who participate in any type of sport are at risk of injury during practices and games. Even the most careful athletes are in danger of injury. Light injuries can be treated through physical therapy or rehabilitation, but there is a high probability for reinjury. Sometimes athletes retire from sport because of chronic injuries. Athletes should try to minimize their risk of injury as much as possible.

Taekwondo demands the use of the entire body, especially the hands and feet. External contusions (bruises) occur frequently. To stay healthy, consider ways to minimize risk and prevent such injuries.

Ordinary taekwondo injuries such as sprains and strains of the instep, toes, ankle, or knee and muscle injuries of the calf, thigh, or hamstrings are often caused by poor practice and drilling habits. Injuries to the thighs, ankles, and knees may occur during practice when the drill level is increased before sufficient warm-up and stretching or when drills are unreasonably intense. Ankle and knee sprains can occur when drills grow more intense.

Poor concentration and excessive muscle tension during practice decrease flexibility. When the intensity of drills increases, the risk of injury also increases. To reduce the risk of injury, sequence practice drills from easy to more difficult and gradually increase speed from slow to fast. Physical fatigue brought on by excessive practice can also cause injury.

It is possible to reduce the risk of injury by promoting flexibility through ample stretching and preparatory drills. Advance from easier to more difficult drills, gradually increasing the level of intensity. Master the basic techniques and use the correct motions and stances. By mastering precise offensive and defensive techniques, you will minimize your risk of injury. Improve muscular power in the whole body through continuous physical exercise. During drills or games, choose sparring drills that are suitable to your physical condition.

When injuries occur, it is important to treat the injured area promptly. First aid means taking temporary measures when a medical specialist is not immediately available. First aid reduces deterioration of the injured part and assists quick recovery.

When an injury occurs, everyone should stay calm. A coach or trainer should try to find out the condition of the patient and the nature of the injury. Others can help to alleviate the patient's anxiety and make the patient comfortable. The coach or trainer should make sure the injured person is breathing easily. For more serious injuries, someone should call an ambulance or transport the patient immediately to the hospital. The coach or trainer should provide an accurate report of the injury to help the doctor understand the situation. At tournament events, usually a medical specialist is available to administer immediate first aid.

For nonemergency injuries, simple first aid can be administered. Begin by assessing the person's condition. Stabilize the injured area and apply ice or a cold compress. Apply compression to the injured area. Help the injured person change to a more comfortable body position, depending on what part of the body is injured and the circumstances of the injury.

Bone fractures can occur through direct or indirect repetitive stimulation due to external shock or excessive practice. Fractures are classified as simple or compound. A broken bone is a medical emergency; seek immediate help from a medical specialist.

Muscular tension is a common symptom of excessive exercise. Part of the muscle stiffens due to persistent use, straining the muscle. If a muscle is sore or tight, try to soften the muscle through massage. Apply a warm, wet towel to the hardened muscle. After about 5 minutes, massage the warm muscle. Repeat every 20 minutes or so until the muscle softens. Repeat for the next two or three days to speed recovery. If pain persists after rest and treatment, seek medical attention.

Contusions (bruises) are caused by external shocks such as collisions or falls. Skin contusions indicate injury to the tissues under the skin or to internal organs. Serious bruises can cause the skin to puff up and turn black and blue. Taekwondo athletes are at risk for foot contusions due to collisions with knees or elbows. Decrease the swelling and pain of bruises to the ankles or insteps with a cold compress. Apply ice or a cold, wet pad four to five times for approximately 20 minutes each time. Depending on the severity of the bruise, application of ice or a cold compress may be continued for two to three days. If ice is not available, put the injured part in cold water. For serious bruises to the head, chest, or stomach, seek immediate help from a medical specialist.

Sprains occur when excessive force is applied to a joint, causing the joint to move in an unnatural direction. The connective tissue around the joint becomes distended or breaks as a result of the excessive extension of the ligament that sustains the joint capsule. Sprains may occur when the intensity of a drill is increased suddenly without proper warm-up or when an athlete is asked to perform a drill that is too advanced. For taekwondo athletes, ankle and foot sprains and bone injuries usually occur to the supporting leg during kicking or footwork. When a foot or ankle is sprained, observe the condition of the injured foot in comparison to the uninjured foot. Swelling and pain are symptoms of a sprain. Recovery from a light sprain can occur within a week. In serious sprains, muscle fibers or soft tissues are torn, causing bleeding within the muscle. Swelling and pain can impair movement in a drill, which may cause reinjury. To prevent reinjury, sufficient rest is required.

As soon as a foot is sprained, apply a layer of foam rubber at the location of the injury and wrap it with an elastic bandage, applying slight pressure to immobilize the joint. Alternatively, treat the joint with ice or a cold pack or dip the foot in ice water. Keep the limb in an elevated position as much as possible. Immobilize the sprained foot to reduce inflammation.

In many sports, ice is used as a first aid tool. In most cases, ice is used as a first measure of treatment for any unexpected injury such as sprains, contusions, and ruptures during training or games. Ice cools the injured part, reducing inflammation and pain and speeding recovery. If ice is not available, use commercial ice packs. Or, soak a towel in ice water, wring the water out, and apply the towel to the injured joint. Leave the towel on for 20 minutes, remove it for 5 minutes, and refresh the towel in ice water and apply again. Continue repetitive treatment for two to three days.

Taping is used to prevent injuries during training or competition. It is also frequently used to prevent injury recurrence. Taekwondo athletes use taping to prevent ankle, instep, and toe injuries during training or competition. The materials required for taping include scissors; fleece pads or layered gauze; sponges or pads made of cotton, gauze, or foam rubber; and petroleum jelly. Athletes who have minor injuries from training may decide to proceed in a competition despite their injuries; therefore, some taping may be required. On a similar note, athletes who are injured during an event may decide to proceed if the injury is minor. In that case, it is wise to seek the advice of the medical professional on staff at the tournament. Make sure you know the rules of the event. In some cases, foam pads may not be allowed for pre-competition injuries.

3

Increasing Strength, Explosive Power, Endurance, and Agility

Taekwondo requires continuous motion for kicking and punching, which requires muscle control. Even simple drills are impossible without basic physical strength plus explosive power and endurance. Points earned in a match are based on accuracy, power, sound, and displacement. Kicks or punches that do not meet those criteria cannot contribute to a win. Understanding that strength, power, endurance, and agility are intimately linked is a key to performing well in the ring.

MUSCULAR STRENGTH

In taekwondo, muscular strength assists in smoothly combining motions such as kicking and punching. Muscular strength is an essential element in taekwondo drills and is directly linked to match outcomes. Muscular strength can be improved through weight training or body weight exercise, either in a group setting or alone.

Strength exercises should be done in sets of 10 repetitions. As strength and endurance improve, more sets can be added.

Begin with rolling push-ups, both forward and backward. Bend over at the waist and place your hands on the floor out about two-thirds of the body's length such that the body is not quite horizontal to the floor but the hips are raised above the chest. Placement of the hands and feet should be about one and a half times the width of the shoulders. Bend your arms at the elbows and lower your chest to the floor in a rolling forward motion followed by hips and knees. As the knees drop, raise the chest and straighten the arms. Reverse the action back to the original position.

After the rolling push-ups, perform sit-ups with your hands crossed over your chest. When you finish the sit-ups, flip over onto your stomach for reverse sit-ups. Clasp your hands behind your back and raise your upper body off the floor. Finish your floor work with leg lifts. Lie on your back and tuck your hands under your hips. While keeping your knees straight, lift your legs.

Once you finish the leg lifts, stand up for rabbit jumps. Begin in a low squat, knees forward, hands over ears. Gently bounce. Stay low to the ground when you bounce. You can either bounce in place or you can move forward as you bounce.

After the rabbit jumps, perform the duck walk. Begin in a low squat, thighs touching calves. Move your right foot forward and then your left foot, maintaining the low squat while moving forward.

Squats are next. Begin by squatting with your feet together. Stand and clasp your hands behind your back. Keep your heels on the floor as you squat slightly. After finishing the squats with the feet together, stand with your feet shoulder-width apart, hands behind your back. Keep your heels on the floor as you squat slightly. Once you finish that set, squat on one foot. Stand up straight, lift one leg off the floor, and slightly squat on the standing leg. You can hold onto a chair or wall for support.

Partner squats are next. Begin by facing your partner, feet shoulder-width apart. You and your partner put your hands on each other's shoulders and both go down into a squat. Next, squat with your partner on your back. With your partner on your back, lean forward slightly. Go down into a shallow squat. Be careful not to squat too deeply.

Aerobic activity rounds out the strength training. Begin by jumping rope. Try to finish 500 jumps each day. After jumping rope, run stairs. If you don't have a flight of stairs handy, you can use a step stool to step up and down, alternating legs to raise the body. Start with sets of 10. Uphill and downhill running is next. During downhill running, slow your pace. For a more intense workout, perform kicks in between steps during the uphill running. Finish by running in place while your partner holds a resistance band around your waist.

EXPLOSIVE POWER

Explosive power is an important element of physical strength. Explosive power enables successful kicking through quickness and force. A fighter with explosive power is like a race car that bursts off the starting line at the wave of the flag.

In taekwondo, explosive power gives fighters the ability to execute a preemptive attack as soon as they detect the opponent's movement to attack. Explosive power is directly linked to winning and losing, so this element of physical strength is required in order to become an excellent athlete.

To develop explosive power, incorporate the following exercises into your training routine:

- Run in place or forward while bringing the knees to waist height and slapping the hands on the knees.
- Perform the frog long jump. Begin in a low squat with hands over ears. Jump forward and extend the body. After landing, return to a low squat and repeat.
- Jump up and bring the knees to the chest.
- Jump up and stretch the legs out to the sides (flying side splits). Reach for the toes.
- Jump up, bringing the feet to the rear. Reach for the toes.
- Jump rope for 500 rotations.
- Alternate fast running with slow walking. Over a distance of 300 feet (91 meters), sprint for approximately 50 feet (15 meters), then slowly walk for about 25 feet (8 meters), then sprint 50 feet again. Repeat this sequence over the 300 feet.
- Sprint and touch down. Set up a course of approximately 30 feet (9 meters). Sprint the 30 feet, bend over, and touch your hand to the ground. Turn, run back to the start, bend over, and touch your hand to the ground. Repeat.
- Run in place while your partner holds a resistance band around your waist.

ENDURANCE

Endurance is the ability to continue performing a repetitive motion that affects breathing, heart rate, and muscular function. When people experience frequent pain in an activity, they often give up. Athletes must improve heart and lung capacity and muscular endurance in order to overcome pain.

Endurance is also related to psychological energy. A person with a strong desire to meet a challenge has a better chance of enduring. Marathon runners who persist to the finish line are an example of strong psychological energy.

If you experience pain during a drill or contest, it may help to visualize yourself successfully completing the drill or contest. Listening to music can help turn your focus away from the pain. Mental concentration directed toward pleasant activities also helps to redirect any focus on pain.

Taekwondo athletes can lose opportunities if lack of endurance causes so much pain that they want to give up a match. Breathing becomes labored and the fighter looks exhausted in the second round because of excessive energy consumption in the first round.

Endurance can be improved through continuous training. A long-term exercise plan incorporating the following activities will increase endurance.

Running activities are good for developing cardiovascular endurance. Long-distance running for 1 to 2 miles (1.6 to 3 kilometers), uphill and downhill running, short-distance circuit running with touchdowns, running up and down stairs, and zigzag running (alternating the feet forward and back while running sideways) are good options for increasing endurance.

Jumping activities also can increase endurance. Try jumping over the back of a partner. This jumping drill can also be done in a group. Begin with one jumper at the back of the line. Everyone else is bent over. The jumper moves forward, leaping over each person. After the last leap, the jumper takes a position at the front of the line. The last person in the line moves forward, jumping over everyone and taking a place at the front of the line. Repeat until everyone has a chance to jump the line.

Jumping drills also can be done without a partner. For example, you might jump side to side over an imaginary line. For more of a challenge, jump side to side over an obstacle on the floor, keeping the feet together.

Taekwondo techniques can be incorporated into endurance training. In front of a mirror or with a partner, mix up steps and sparring motions as quickly as you can. Try a kicking-bag workout using speed kicks or double kicks. Move onto kicks with a partner. Exchange different kicks with your partner nonstop for a set time limit or number of kicks. Try step sparring for two rounds, two minutes per round, with no contact. Concentrate on footwork and your reaction to your partner. Finish with paddle sparring. Have your partner hold paddles and quickly present them in different positions.

Any extracurricular aerobic activity, such as soccer or basketball, can also improve endurance and provide a fun break from regular training.

AGILITY

Agility is the ability of the fighter to control the body while maintaining power and speed. Step sparring will improve agility and reflexes. Other activities for improving agility are running in place, zigzag running, speed kicks, sideways running in small steps, paddle sparring, and sports such as soccer and basketball.

Without agility, effective attack and counterattack skills cannot be performed with speed. Agility is the ability to move quickly, shift weight, and move back and forth and side to side as necessary in the ring. When athletes decide to compete in a younger age class (usually allowed in local tournaments), they are often surprised to find that their agility and reaction times are somewhat slower than the agility and reaction times of their younger competitors. Agility and speed change as athletes get older, which is one of the reasons there are age divisions in competition.

CIRCUIT AND INTERVAL TRAINING

Circuit training with weightlifting is recommended in addition to taekwondo training. The purpose of circuit training is to strengthen and improve function

Body control is a crucial skill for a fighter.

for specific parts of the body. Through repeated exercise or repetitions using focus methods, individual components of the body can be strengthened.

Generally, a circuit includes exercises for the arms, neck, shoulders, stomach, waist, legs, and back. Each drill has a specific time limit such as 30 or 60 seconds in which the athlete performs a prescribed number of repetitions or sets. Once the sets are complete, the athlete moves on to the next drill. The goal is either to increase the number of repetitions that can be performed within the time limit or to shorten the time limit while completing the same number of repetitions.

Circuit training can be incorporated into a taekwondo athlete's training plan in a variety of ways. Here is a sample circuit designed to improve muscular strength, muscular endurance, agility, reaction time, and flexibility.

Physical Training

Develops muscular strength, endurance, and power.

- Jump rope—2 minutes
- Stretching—5 to 10 minutes
- Push-ups—1 minute or 50 repetitions
- Sit-ups—1 minute or 50 repetitions
- Squats—1 minute or 50 repetitions

- Duck walk—1 or 2 minutes
- Resistance running in place—1 or 2 minutes
- Jumping in place, knees to chest—1 minute or 20 repetitions
- Short-distance running with touchdowns—10 sets
- Squat jumps, starting low and bouncing without reaching full height—10 repetitions
- Side-step shuffle—5 minutes

Kicking Drills

Develop muscular and cardiovascular endurance and speed.

- Pulling-step front kick, round kick back and forth with partner for 30 or 60 seconds, then move on to the next kick without rest.
- Pulling-step front kick, side kick back and forth with partner for 30 or 60 seconds, then move on to the next kick without rest.
- Pulling-step front kick, hook kick, or axe kick with partner for 30 or 60 seconds.

Paddle Drills

Develop muscular and cardiovascular endurance, power control, and accuracy.

- With kicker in the middle and two partners holding paddles, kicker uses basic kicks without steps or punches for 30 to 60 seconds.
- With kicker in the middle and two partners holding paddles, kicker uses basic kicks with steps but without punches for 30 to 60 seconds.
- With one person holding the paddle, the kicker moves through the paddle, back and forth, executing a skill such as a pushing kick, axe kick, or punch through the paddle.

The purpose of interval training is to improve stamina while increasing speed and endurance. Both interval training and circuit training should be part of a long-term training plan.

With interval training, the athlete moves from a higher intensity activity to a lower intensity activity instead of taking a break between drills. This helps to build whole-body endurance, which is required during the continuous offensive and defensive actions in a match.

One suggestion for interval training is light running. On a flat surface, jump 20 to 30 times, bringing the knees to the chest, then sprint 50 feet (15 meters) at full speed. Walk a short distance and repeat. On a hilly road, run full speed uphill and run slowly downhill. Finally, try sprinting at full speed for 50 to 100 feet (15 to 30 meters), walking a short distance, and then sprinting 50 to 100 feet again. Repetition will build strength and endurance.

4

Kicking and Blocking

The foundation of taekwondo is kicks and punches. Basic kicks can be used for attacks and counterattacks and can be adjusted for short- or long-distance targets. Punches can supplement a kicking strategy in counterattacking an opponent. For example, if the opponent launches an attack and you fail to dodge it, move in close with a punching defense and follow up with a kick. Accurate, powerful kicks will give you the proper countermeasures to use in varying circumstances.

At the start of a kick, the body weight usually is on the nonkicking leg. The body weight is transferred to the striking leg in the direction of the target. The knees are always flexed. They act as shock absorbers and allow you to pivot on the supporting foot.

Visualize the target of the kick and set the direction of the strike. Concentrate in order to follow through any kicking maneuver.

With the target in sight, control the distance to the target with sliding or running footwork. (See chapter 5 on steps.) You may have to shuffle in, take a running quick step to close a gap, or take steps to the back or side to position yourself for the attack. Lift the knee for the strike and readjust your body to the target. Resist planting your feet flat on the floor. Keep your heels slightly off the floor. This helps you pivot when launching the kick and rechambering your leg for the next move.

Always rechamber your leg quickly so that you are prepared for the next attack or counterattack. For example, if you leave your striking leg in post-strike position, your body will be open to a strike from your opponent.

Rechambering your leg to the starting position also helps remove your torso from the opponent's striking range. Stay in a slightly lowered stance, keeping your knees bent and flexible.

Repetition of kick mechanics—weight shift, balance, stance, quickness, powerful delivery, foot position, distance control—helps ingrain the kick into muscle memory. During practice, you may find it helpful to support your body with something stable. When training, be sure to execute kicks with all components of the kick in mind.

BASIC KICKS

For each basic kick, there is a striking point, target, and direction. The striking point is the part of the foot that makes contact with the target. Remember, points are scored by contact with the foot, below the ankle only. Contact with the shin or knee will not result in a point. The following descriptions list the targets that are the most common focus for each kicking technique. As with any kick, a torso score is worth only 1 point, whereas a kick to the head or face earns 2 points. Kicks below the ho gu are illegal and will result in a penalty call from the referee. The direction of the kick refers to the relationship of the kick to the opponent's torso.

Front Snap Kick

Striking point: Ball of foot

Target: Trunk, side, ribs, face

Direction: Straight

The front snap kick is used less often in sparring than other kicks. Since round kicks are used often, a simultaneous snap kick and opponent's round kick usually result in crashing of the knees. Another downside is that when executing a snap kick, your torso is vulnerable to a back kick. You could use a snap as a fake, such as a quick, low snap of the foot immediately blended into a round kick. If you are quick, a high snap kick to your opponent's chin might earn you 2 points. For the most part, the snap kick has evolved into a pushing kick when it comes to the ring.

For the front snap kick, lift the striking leg in bent-knee position (figure 4.1a). The height of the knee will direct the kick. For a high kick, lift the knee to a high position; for a low kick, use a low knee position. Lean back slightly, staying balanced on the supporting leg. Leaning backward promotes a longer reach and greater kicking height.

Use your knee to spring the lower leg forward (figure 4.1b). Curl your toes upward and strike with the ball of your foot. The supporting leg will also spring upward when the kick is launched. Keep the supporting leg slightly bent at the knee to maintain balance. The heel of the nonkicking leg will come slightly off the floor, and the foot will pivot to help you keep balance. Quickly rechamber your leg in preparation for the next motion.

a   *b*

Figure 4.1   Front snap kick: *(a)* raise the striking leg, bending the knee; *(b)* snap the knee to execute the kick.

Roundhouse Kick

Striking point: Instep of foot

Target: Trunk, side, ribs, face

Direction: Side

The roundhouse kick is used about 70 percent of the time in the sparring ring in either attacks or counterattacks. The roundhouse kick is fast and is easily combined with other kicks. The roundhouse is a high-scoring kick.

Bring the striking leg up in bent-knee position (figure 4.2*a*). The height of the knee will direct the kick. For a high kick, lift the knee to a high position; for a low kick, use a low knee position. The ball of the nonkicking foot will pivot slightly to turn the torso and roll the hip forward. Lean back slightly at the torso, hip forward. Balance on the supporting leg, keeping the supporting knee flexed.

Use a springing action with the lower leg to kick the target (figure 4.2*b*), striking the target with the instep of the foot, not the shin. After the strike, rechamber the leg by bending the leg back to the bent-knee position (figure 4.2*c*) and then quickly extending the leg to the starting position (figure 4.2*d*).

Figure 4.2 Roundhouse kick: *(a)* raise kicking leg with bent knee; *(b)* spring kicking leg forward, striking target with instep; *(c)* rechamber by lowering the leg back to bent-knee position; *(d)* return to ready position.

Side Kick

Striking point: Heel or outside edge of foot

Target: Trunk, ribs, face

Direction: Side (useful when torso is sideways)

Side kicks are seldom used in competition. The side kick rotates the body, making it difficult to combine with other kicks. In addition, your opponent should be able to easily lean away from a side kick.

Bring the striking leg up in a bent-knee position (figure 4.3*a*). The height of the knee will direct the kick. For a high kick, lift the knee to a high position; for a low kick, use a low knee position. Bring the rear leg forward in a half-circle motion (figure 4.3*b*). Elevate the bent leg so that the knee is slightly lower than the foot. The supporting leg will pivot 180 degrees in the opposite direction of the kick. The torso and hip roll forward.

Extend the kicking leg fully from the hip (figure 4.3*c*). Keep the foot parallel to the floor so you can use the heel or the outside edge of the foot for the strike. The power of the kick comes from the hip. The torso is angled in the opposite direction of the strike. The extended leg and torso should be about parallel with the floor. Keep the supporting leg flexed to facilitate balance and pivoting.

Quickly rechamber to the starting position by retracting the leg to a bent position and pivoting on the supporting foot, which should bring you back to facing the target (figure 4.3*d*). Bring the body up and forward and return the leg to the starting position (figure 4.3*e*).

a *b*

c *d* *e*

Figure 4.3 Side kick: *(a)* raise kicking leg, knee bent; *(b)* rotate on supporting leg; *(c)* extend leg to execute the kick; *(d)* quickly rechamber leg by bringing in back to bent-knee position, facing opponent; *(e)* return to ready position.

Spin Back Kick

Striking point: Heel

Target: Trunk, face

Direction: Back 180 degrees

The spin back kick is a strong scoring kick and counterattack kick, but it requires a fast rechambering of the kicking leg. The spin back kick is used about 70 percent of the time in the sparring ring in either attacks or counterattacks.

Pivot on the supporting leg. With the back of the heel pointed toward the target, turn the body and view the target over the shoulder on the kicking-leg side (figure 4.4a). Bend the supporting knee. Raise the kicking foot to knee height (figure 4.4b) and extend the leg straight back, passing the foot next to the knee of the supporting leg (figure 4.4c). Extend the torso over the supporting leg and lean forward. Thrust the kicking leg back toward the target. Do not use a sweeping motion.

a

Rechamber the leg by quickly retracting the extended leg to a bent position and then turning the body around to face the target.

b

c

Figure 4.4   Spin back kick: *(a)* back of heel points toward opponent; *(b)* lift kicking foot to knee height; *(c)* extend leg straight back to execute kick.

Down Axe Kick, Rear Leg

Striking point: Heel or bottom of foot

Target: Trunk, face

Direction: Straight and down

When facing an opponent who prefers to attack, the down axe kick could make the difference in the match. When the opponent rushes in, the down axe can stop her in her tracks. The target is usually the face; a hit results in 2 points. If the opponent is really rocked off her feet, the standing-down rule earns an additional point. The down axe kick requires flexibility and the ability to extend the leg high and close. Because the torso is vulnerable while the leg is in the air, the down axe kick must be executed quickly.

a *b*

Figure 4.5 Down axe kick: *(a)* begin in ready position; *(b)* bring the rear leg forward, keeping the leg straight.

For the rear-leg approach, swing the stiff, straight leg to the opponent's head (figure 4.5). Point the toes to strike with the bottom of the foot or flex the foot for a heel strike. Bring the leg straight down while the leg is still outstretched.

Half-Moon (Crescent) Kick

Striking point: Bottom of foot

Target: Face

Direction: Across

The half-moon, or crescent, kick is good for blocking punches or closing distances. If you have the ability to raise the leg in a full, upright, up-close extension, this kick works well in a clinch. As with the down axe kick, strong abdominal muscles help to bring the leg up high and close, resulting in 2 points for a facial attack.

When you're really close to your opponent or in a clinch, raise a slightly bent leg, as if hooking, from the rear. Aim for your opponent's head. Point the toes for a strike with the bottom of the foot or flex the foot for a heel strike. Sweep the leg in a half-circle for an outside-to-inside strike or raise the leg in a sweeping, half-circle motion from just in front of the supporting leg for an inside-to-outside strike (figure 4.6). Quickly rechamber the leg to the rear.

a   *b*   *c*

d   *e*

Figure 4.6   Half-moon kick: *(a)* begin in ready position; *(b)* raise rear leg, slightly bent; *(c)* sweep leg in a half-circle, aiming for opponent's head; *(d)* bring kicking leg around; *(e)* return to ready position.

Hook Kick

Striking point: Bottom of foot

Target: Face

Direction: Across

The hook kick, rear or front, is used mostly for attacking. It's easy to front-load a fake such as a cut kick or low snap and then combine it with the hook. The opponent might then block the low kick and be unprepared for the hook.

Pivot the supporting foot to the outside. Bend the knee, as in a roundhouse kick, and raise the leg to target level (figure 4.7*a*). Lean sideways so that the torso is angled in the opposite direction of the kick (figure 4.7*b*). Launch the kick from the bottom half of the leg. The upper thigh more or less stays in the same position. While the bent leg is still in the air, kick from the knee, not from the hip (figure 4.7*c*). Power is generated by the waist and hip. The kick can be short and quick, like snapping at the target. Look at the target and sweep the foot across it. Quickly rechamber the leg in the starting position.

a　　　　　*b*　　　　　*c*

Figure 4.7　Hook kick: *(a)* lift knee to target level; *(b)* extend leg toward face and angle torso in opposite direction of the kick; *(c)* execute the kick from the knee, not the hip.

Spin Hook Kick

Striking point: Heel or bottom of foot

Target: Face

Direction: Back and across

a

The spin hook kick requires balance and speed. It is a great kick for knockouts and is mostly used for counterattacks.

Pivot on the front foot. Turn backward with the heel pointed toward the opponent as if you were executing a back kick. Turn the torso and view the target over your shoulder (figure 4.8*a*). Locate your opponent with a quick glance. You must be fast and accurate. Turn your head quickly and the body will follow.

Bend the knee of the supporting leg. Raise the kicking leg and bend it at the knee (figure 4.8*b*). Move the leg to the rear while raising the leg at the hip.

Lean forward at the waist. Bring the bent leg around and snap kick from the knee for a strike with the bottom of the foot (figure 4.8*c*). Generate power at the waist while spinning. Quickly extend the leg for the strike.

b

c

Figure 4.8   Spin hook kick: *(a)* heel points at opponent, view opponent over shoulder; *(b)* extend the leg toward the face; *(c)* snap knee to execute the kick.

Alternatively, you can use a more sweeping, curving motion. Use the whole leg, generating power from the hip, while still snapping the kick at the knee. Quickly rechamber the leg. The complete execution resembles a full circle as you return to the starting position.

ADVANCED KICKS

For each advanced kick, a striking point, target, and direction are listed. As with the basic kicks, the striking point is the part of the foot used for impact, the target refers to the most common focus for a kick, and the direction refers to the general relationship of the kick to the opponent's torso.

Down Front Axe Kick, Front Foot

Striking point: Heel or bottom of foot

Target: Trunk, face

Direction: Straight and down

The down front axe kick is used as a counterattack in close situations or to stop an opponent's momentum. If you have enough distance, swing a stiff, straight leg to your opponent's head (figure 4.9). Point your toes and strike with the bottom of your foot or flex your foot for a heel strike. Bring your outstretched leg straight down.

For a close-range kick, perhaps stopping the momentum of an opponent, slide your front foot slightly toward your rear foot. Lift the kicking knee to a bent position close to your chest. Extend the bottom half of your kicking leg in a light, downward strike. There is no need to strike with force as the bottom of the foot will stop any forward momentum. To make this kick work you must have the ability to raise the straight leg close to your body.

a   *b*

Figure 4.9   Down front axe kick: *(a)* begin in ready position; *(b)* swing a straight leg at the opponent's head.

Counter Rear Round Kick With Bada Chagi (Twist Step)

Striking point: Instep
Target: Trunk, ribs, or face
Direction: Sideways

This round kick with a twist step (figure 4.10) will allow you to move off to the side more quickly than a side step. Slide your front foot sideways in front and to the inside of your body about 45 degrees out of your opponent's line of forward motion. Replace your rear foot with your front foot. With a slight jump as your feet switch positions, launch a rear-leg strike. This is one of the most common kicks used for counterattack. (Refer to chapter 5 for more on steps.)

a
b
c

d
e

Figure 4.10   Counter rear round kick: *(a)* begin in ready position; *(b)* jump to switch feet; *(c)* bring rear foot forward; *(d)* land and extend kicking leg; *(e)* execute kick.

Jump Spin Back Kick

Striking point: Heel

Target: Trunk, face

Direction: Straight back

The jump spin back kick is the same as a spin back kick, except the kick is initiated from a stationary position without the placing of the pivot foot. The jump spin back kick is used about 70 percent of the time in the sparring ring in either attacks or counterattacks. The jump spin back kick is a high-scoring counterattack kick.

The technique for the jump spin back kick is the same as the technique for the spin back kick, only there are no steps. The kick is executed in place as you jump and must be performed extremely quickly if it is to be effective. The turning of the torso telegraphs your intentions. The opponent shouldn't have time to react or you will find that you are an open target.

Quickly turn your head and torso 180 degrees to view your target over your kicking-leg shoulder (figure 4.11a). Bend your supporting knee and jump (figure 4.11b), extending your kicking leg straight back toward your target (figure 4.11c). Rechamber your leg quickly by retracting the extended leg to a bent position. Turn around to face your target.

a   *b*   *c*

Figure 4.11   Jump spin back kick: *(a)* look over shoulder at opponent; *(b)* quickly bend supporting knee and jump; *(c)* extend kicking leg to target.

Jump Spin Hook Kick

Striking point: Heel or bottom of foot

Target: Face

Direction: Sweeping and to the back, as if slapping the face with the bottom of the foot

The technique for the jump spin hook kick is the same as for the jump spin back kick except the striking leg doesn't go straight back. Instead the striking leg hooks for a sweeping strike.

Bend your supporting knee and jump, extending your kicking leg slightly off center of your target. Rechamber your leg quickly by retracting the extended leg to a bent position (figure 4.12*a*). Turn around and face your target. As in a regular hook kick, raise the kicking leg (figure 4.12*b*) and bend at the knee. Move the leg to the rear while raising the leg at the hip. Bend forward at the waist, focus on the target, and bring the bent leg around. Snap the kick from the knee for a strike with the bottom of the foot (figure 4.12*c*).

a

b

c

Figure 4.12   Jump spin hook kick: *(a)* jump and retract leg to bent-knee position; *(b)* raise the kicking leg; *(c)* snap knee to execute kick.

Pulling-Step Front Round Kick (Fast Kick)

Striking point: Instep

Target: Trunk, ribs, face

Direction: Side

The pulling-step front round kick, or fast kick, is used to counterattack when the opponent is retreating. It is a high-percentage scoring kick and a good one to

use if you need a fast kick. Although the pulling step is used mostly with a roundhouse kick, the principle can be applied to other kicks.

Slide the rear foot forward toward the front foot (figure 4.13*a*). Shift balance from the front foot to the rear foot. (When switching feet, you can use a slight hop.) As soon as you switch feet, execute the kick. Elevate the knee quickly for a front round kick (figure 4.13*b*). During the kick, lean the upper body backward slightly (figure 4.13*c*). After the kick, quickly rechamber the leg to the starting position.

a

b

c

Figure 4.13   Pulling-step front round kick: *(a)* bring rear foot toward front foot; *(b)* after switching feet, elevate knee for kick; *(c)* while executing the kick, lean upper body back slightly.

Hop-Step Front Axe Kick

Striking point: Bottom of the foot

Target: Trunk, face

Direction: Straight and down

The hop-step front axe kick (figure 4.14) is a long-distance technique. The hop step can also be used with round kicks.

With your rear foot, take one step forward past your front foot but do not place your foot on the floor. Instead, place your foot on an imaginary box on the floor and use this box to launch the kick with the other leg, as in a jump kick. The supporting leg is slightly bent. Raise the knee to your chest while bounding upward to launch the kick. Lean the upper body backward slightly when launching the kick. Balance is important. Quickly rechamber the kicking leg and slide back to the starting position.

Alternatively, you can replace the front foot with the rear foot or move forward to close the gap before striking at the target. This technique can also be used without the jump.

a

b

c

d

Figure 4.14   Hop-step front axe kick: *(a)* step rear foot past front foot; *(b)* jump; *(c)* raise knee to chest; *(d)* launch kick.

Double or Triple Round Kick

Striking point: Instep

Target: Trunk, ribs, face, legs

Direction: Side

The double or triple round kick can be used for short- or long-range targets.

The rear leg comes forward, moving in front of the front foot, and lands on an imaginary box. Slightly jump off the front foot, elevating the bent leg in a 30-degree plane. At the same time, the supporting foot pivots slightly to turn the torso and roll the hip forward. Lean the torso back slightly and balance on the supporting leg, keeping the knee flexed. You can also use a fast kick. If your opponent retreats, don't lean back; this will shorten your reach. Maintain your forward motion with the torso upright until you close the distance, then lean back at the last moment.

When combining kicks, the first kick is usually a faking motion while the second kick is the point strike. Do not rechamber the leg to the floor after the first kick; rather, keep the kicking leg in the air.

In a double round kick (figure 4.15), the first kick can be low, below the knee, with the second kick to the trunk, or the first kick can be to the trunk with the second kick to the face. In a triple round kick, use the first and second kicks to move up your opponent's body like stair steps, with a third strike to the face.

a

b *c* *d*

Figure 4.15 Double round kick: *(a)* lift bent knee; *(b)* execute first kick; *(c)* jump; *(d)* execute second kick.

Tornado (Turn) Kick

Striking point: Instep
Target: Trunk, ribs, face
Direction: 360 degrees to the side

For the tornado kick, you will be turning 180 degrees. Including the rechambering of the leg after the kick, this technique will take you in a full circle.

Switch your body position 180 degrees by turning clockwise while moving one step forward. At the same time, pivot on your supporting leg and rotate your head to view your target over your shoulder (figure 4.16a). Bring the rear leg around in a half-circle (figure 4.16b) and with a slight jump (figure 4.16c) replace the front foot, either in the same position or slightly forward if you need to close a gap. The jump helps you launch the front foot in a round kick (figure 4.16d). Although jumping is mostly used for round kicks, it can be incorporated into other kicks such as axe or pushing kicks.

The same kick can be executed without a jump, essentially leaving your feet on the floor as you rotate your body.

Always keep your knees flexed and quickly rechamber the kick. At this point you will have come full circle (360 degrees).

a

b   c   d

Figure 4.16   Tornado kick: (a) pivot on supporting leg and look over shoulder at opponent; (b) bring rear leg around; (c) jump; (d) launch round kick with front foot.

Reverse Tornado Kick

Striking point: Instep

Target: Trunk, ribs, face

Direction: 360 degrees to the side

The reverse tornado kick takes the inside clockwise approach. The front foot moves back, only you step inside or clockwise, crossing your front foot in front of your rear leg as if turning your back on your opponent.

Plant your left foot to the rear and then pivot both feet so your torso is turned to your opponent. Once you are facing your opponent, execute a left roundhouse kick, a crescent kick, or a down axe kick. Speed is of the essence.

The tornado kick can be executed with a jump. Instead of planting the left foot to the rear, pretend you are planting it on an imaginary box. Rotate your body, keeping your foot in the air and leaning your upper body back slightly. With a slight jump, execute a rear strike with your left leg.

Pushing Kick

Striking point: Bottom of foot

Target: Trunk, ribs, hip

Direction: Straight

The pushing kick (figure 4.17) is mainly used to stop an opponent's forward motion and create an opportunity for the next motion in the attack immediately following the kick. This kick evolved as a better solution to the snap kick. A good foot plant on the chest pad could send an opponent reeling.

Figure 4.17 Pushing kick: *(a)* begin in ready position.

a

(continued)

b   **c**

Figure 4.17   Pushing kick *(continued): (b)* raise leg; *(c)* lean back and thrust leg forward to stop opponent's forward momentum.

Raise your leg in a snap, front-kick position. Select a target (focus on the opponent's hip, trunk, or ribs if you want to stop your opponent's forward motion). You can use either a front-leg approach or a rear-leg approach. If you choose a rear-leg approach, you may need to skip forward to close the gap to your opponent.

Lean back and thrust your bent leg straight forward in a pushing motion against your opponent. If you are close to your opponent, keep your body upright and pull your knee to your chest before thrusting the leg forward for the kick.

Cut Kick

Striking point: Bottom of foot

Target: Trunk, ribs, hip

Direction: Side

The cut kick is similar to the pushing kick. The cut kick is most often used to stop an opponent's forward motion, but it also can be used as a feint motion or to stop an opponent's attack. It is a good kick to use when initiating a combination kick such as cut–spin back kick, cut–spin hook kick, cut–double round kick, cut–tornado kick, and so on. The basic technique is the same as for a pushing kick, only the body doesn't have a straightforward orientation. Cut kicks don't score points and generally are not used with striking force. The cut kick is not a true kick; it could be considered an air kick (like air guitar). Mostly it is used in faking an action, as in raising the leg up in a cut action, or by planting or touching the foot on the opponent before executing a combination kick. The motion of the cut kick mimics other kicks and therefore can be used to fool the opponent about your intentions.

The front cut kick is usually targeted at the hip, trunk, ribs, or face. Stay in the same spot and lean back (figure 4.18). Raise your front foot to stop your opponent or lean back and raise your front leg, skipping forward on your rear leg, and stop your opponent with your front foot. Raise your leg halfway and flex your foot, making contact with the bottom of your foot. For a rear-leg strike, cut step and then rechamber your leg. In either case, body position can be slightly sideways or forward.

Figure 4.18 For a front cut kick, lean back and raise your leg to stop your opponent.

The targets for a rear cut kick (figure 4.19) are the same as for the front cut kick. Bring your rear leg forward in a cut motion. Lean back and raise your knee. Flex your foot up and make contact with the bottom of your foot. Alternatively you can bring your rear leg forward in a cut motion, drop down, and switch feet (front to back or back to front). Another option is to bring your rear leg forward in a cut motion, skip forward on your supporting leg, raise your knee, and push your opponent with your foot.

a   *b*   *c*

Figure 4.19 Rear cut kick: *(a)* move rear leg forward; *(b)* lean back and raise knee; *(c)* execute kick.

The hop-step front cut kick (figure 4.20) involves a little more action than simply raising the leg. Bring your rear foot forward to the front foot as in a pulling step. Shift your weight to your rear foot and raise the front foot in a cut kick. You can perform this step more than once, executing a back-and-forth rocking motion.

a   b

Figure 4.20   Hop-step front cut kick: *(a)* move rear foot forward; *(b)* raise front foot for a cut kick.

A word of caution is in order here. A penalty could be called if the cut lands anywhere below the legal area of the ho gu. It is important to quickly combine the cut with another kick unless you are just fishing for a reaction.

BLOCKING AND PUNCHING

Blocking and punching are used when two opponents are close to each other. If you execute a kick but your opponent doesn't move, use a punch to budge your opponent and give yourself a chance to place a scoring kick. If your opponent is attacking and you are close, block your opponent's kick and follow with a punch to give yourself a chance to create the distance you need to execute a scoring kick.

Punches seldom result in points during a match. Remember, punches to the face are illegal. Visual displacement of the opponent along with an obvious sound upon impact might generate a point from the referees. However, punches are usually buried in solid kick techniques and don't get much attention.

Here are some common competitive blocks and punches:

- From a fighting stance, slide the left foot forward or 45 degrees to the side until you are in a front stance. Follow with your right foot. With your left arm, block your opponent's rear-leg kick. With your right fist, deliver a punch at the same time (figure 4.21*a*). Keep your body weight forward. Throw your weight into the punch.

- From a fighting stance, slide your left foot forward and 45 degrees to the side until you are in a front stance. Block your opponent's front kick with your right arm and follow up with a punch with your left fist (figure 4.21*b*). Keep your body weight forward. Throw your weight into the punch.

- For a defensive block, use one palm to block your face (figure 4.21*c*) and the other palm to block your body.

- If your opponent tries a back kick and you have no time for a counter-kick, fold both arms flat over your stomach to block the impact of your opponent's kick (figure 4.21*d*).

- If you opponent tries an axe or a crescent kick, raise your arm straight up and bend it slightly at the elbow to block the kick (figure 4.21*e*).

a *b*

Figure 4.21 Common blocks and punches used in competition: *(a)* block opponent's kick with left arm, punch with right fist; *(b)* block opponent's front kick with right arm, punch with left fist.

(continued)

c

d

e

f

Figure 4.21   Common blocks and punches used in competition *(continued): (c)* use palm to block face; *(d)* fold arms over abdomen to block opponent's back kick; *(e)* raise arm to block opponent's high kick; *(f)* hold arms straight down in a double low block.

- As a defensive block, put both arms down in a double low block (figure 4.21*f*). Twist your body for the block as necessary.
- In a clinch, put both arms straight out to block the upward motion of an impending axe kick.

5

Stepping and Footwork

Steps are used to feint motions, adjust distance, and execute combinations. By taking preemptive steps, you may be able to block or disrupt your opponent's attack and gain the upper hand. Steps also create time for you to analyze your opponent's movements. Well-timed steps will help you carry out effective attacks and defense.

In this chapter, we discuss four basic methods of movement in the ring: steps in place, steps forward, steps to the side, and steps back. These techniques offer a full range of strategies to accommodate any kind of fighting style. The various stepping procedures lead you through the match in a prescribed, thought-out method as opposed to just jumping around the ring without a plan.

In this chapter, a closed stance means that both competitors are standing with the left foot forward (to the front) and the right foot back (to the rear).

STEPS IN PLACE

Steps in place are simply steps in which the body does not move forward, to the side, or back. These steps may help you change your position from closed to open, confuse the opponent, elicit a response, or set yourself up for a spin kick. In each case, bounding in place, switching feet, and switching feet with scissor action are accomplished without changing position on the mat.

Bounding in Place

Bounding in place is simply bouncing on the balls of the feet while keeping the body weight on the balls of the feet (figure 5.1). The continuous movement while bounding serves several purposes. First, the balance of the torso is easily thrust forward or backward as necessary, thus making it easier to initiate an attack or react with a counterattack. Second, the illusion of constant movement makes it more difficult for an opponent to read your next move. Imagine standing completely still and then suddenly thrusting forward to launch an attack. Your movement would be boldly telegraphed to the opponent. The slight movements involved in bounding don't give the opponent this signal. Small faking motions are usually incorporated into bounding so that the real attack is disguised. Third, bounding keeps the joints flexible.

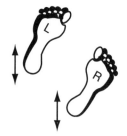

Bounding on the balls of the feet.

a   *b*

Figure 5.1   Bounding in place: *(a)* knees are bent; *(b)* bounce on the balls of the feet.

For forward motion with a rear-leg kick (attack position), begin by bouncing on the balls of the feet. Keep your knees bent. Shift your weight forward to the front foot. Follow through as your body weight shifts forward, providing power for the rear-leg kick when attacking. Note: Any number of kicks can be used, such as a roundhouse, axe, or pushing kick.

A backward motion will put you in counterattack position. Bounce on the balls of the feet, keeping the knees bent. Shift your body weight to your rear foot. Lean back slightly and strike with your front or rear foot or execute a jump spin kick. Note: Any number of kicks can be used, even a back kick.

Switching Feet

Use the switch-foot step to change body position (figure 5.2). This step is good for counterattacks involving spin back, spin hook, or rear-leg kicks. Switching the direction of the torso can confuse the opponent or draw the opponent in. If you know that the opponent favors a particular kick for which you have a good combination counter, then switching feet may cause the opponent to initiate the kick, which is precisely the objective. Finally, in the process of switching feet, you can alter the distance between yourself and your opponent as needed.

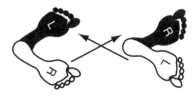

Switch-foot step.

a   b   c

Figure 5.2   Switch-foot step: *(a)* begin in a balanced, low stance; *(b)* slide front foot to the rear and rear foot to the front; *(c)* change direction.

Stand in a balanced, lower stance. Keep the heels off the floor. Switch the position of your feet; slide your front foot to the rear and your rear foot to the front. Make sure your whole body follows; change the direction of your stance from open to closed or closed to open. Shift your weight forward for a forward kick or backward for a counterkick. Follow up with a front- or rear-leg kick.

The kicks most frequently used with this step are roundhouse kicks, pushing kicks, cut kicks, or kicking combinations. If you are switching feet for a counterattack, be careful; you may give your opponent a chance to attack. Be prepared to launch a spin kick.

Switching Feet With Scissor Action

In this step, you switch the position of your feet without changing your body position. Reverse the position of your feet but do not change the direction of your body (figure 5.3). Keep your weight centered over your feet. Your front foot moves to the rear, and you can launch a forward kick. The action of switching feet helps to propel the body forward. This step is used as an attacking step with a rear-foot pushing kick, roundhouse kick, or axe kick. You can also incorporate a fake. For example, the rear foot starts to move forward but shifts to the side instead. This step can also be used to control distance.

a   *b*

Figure 5.3   Switching feet, scissor action: *(a)* begin in a balanced stance; *(b)* bring the rear foot forward and the front foot back without changing direction.

STEPS FORWARD

In forward steps, the stepping motions have subtle differences, but in each case, the objective is to move forward. These steps are considered attacking steps. There are six different methods for forward motion: forward shuffle step, rear-leg skip step, fast-kick step, one step forward, running (quick) step, and 180-degree forward step. Each step is unique; some movements are subtle and others are more obvious. You can control distance, create visual confusion, inject speed, or project a fake in the ring by using forward steps.

Forward Shuffle Step

A forward shuffle (figure 5.4) is good for controlling timing and distance for an attack. The forward motion should also elicit a natural reaction from your opponent, which is what you want. You can create visual confusion for the opponent by using the whole body to fake a forward motion.

Forward shuffle, rear foot first.

a   *b*   *c*

Figure 5.4   Forward shuffle step, front foot first: *(a)* step with the front foot; *(b)* bring the front foot down; *(c)* slide the rear foot forward.

When executing a shuffle step, maintain your balance and keep your body weight centered over your feet. Bend your knees and lower your stance as you lift your heels slightly off the floor. This will provide maximum acceleration. Cover the distance necessary to close the gap to your opponent using either short or long strides.

You can perform shuffle steps in different ways. You can shuffle forward with both feet, with the front foot and rear foot moving simultaneously. You can shuffle forward by stepping with the rear foot first, advancing the rear foot and then sliding the front foot forward an equal distance (shown in the footwork illustration). You can shuffle forward by stepping with the front foot first and then sliding the rear foot forward an equal distance (shown in figure 5.4). In any case, the steps appear as a single, fluid movement when executed correctly, each step blending into the next.

Rear-Leg Skip Step

The rear-leg skip step features a front-foot cut kick and a skipping rear-leg step (figure 5.5). The front leg is used for an attack with a cut kick. The front leg is elevated as the supporting leg skips forward. This forward motion is good for executing a front-foot fake with a rear-leg follow-up or can be combined with a roundhouse, pushing, or axe kick. Lean back slightly.

Kick

Rear-leg skip step.

a   b

Figure 5.5 Rear-leg skip step: *(a)* elevate the front leg as the rear leg skips forward; *(b)* execute a kick.

The rear-leg skip step can also feature a cut kick with the rear leg and a skipping front foot. Sweep the rear leg forward while skipping on the supporting leg. Execute a cut kick. This forward motion is good for executing a fake or for leading into a jump combination (cut–round, cut–axe, and so on) in case your opponent retreats. This step also is good for a long reach. It requires excellent balance on the supporting leg to be effective.

Fast-Kick Step (Pulling Step)

The fast-kick step is used with a front-foot kick and is also referred to as a pulling step or fast step. Think of the fast step as your front-wheel drive. The fast step can be used to close a short or long distance to an opponent or to avoid an attack. Depending on how this step is executed, it can be interpreted by the opponent as a rear-leg kick when in fact it is a front-foot kick. The action of bringing the rear leg forward may signal to the opponent that a rear-leg attack is coming. If the opponent is executing a fast kick, your knees will crash unless you follow through with the fast step and front-leg kick.

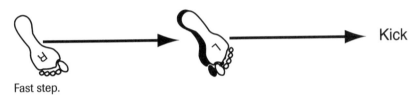

Fast step.

To close a long distance to an opponent, assume a sparring stance with your weight centered over your feet. Slide your rear foot up to your front foot and prepare for a front-leg kick (figure 5.6a). At the same time, shift your body weight forward. As soon as your rear foot touches your front foot, shift your body weight back slightly. Lift your knee and, using a slight jump, move your rear foot forward to replace your front foot (figure 5.6b) as you launch a front-leg strike in one smooth motion (figure 5.6c).

a   b   c

Figure 5.6 Fast-kick step: *(a)* bring rear foot to front foot and shift weight forward; *(b)* lift knee of front leg; *(c)* execute a front-leg kick.

If your opponent is using a rear-leg kick, counterattack with a fast kick using a short axe, roundhouse, pushing, or cut kick or faking motion. The fast step is also a good option when an opponent hesitates or shows no reaction, giving you the chance to execute a quick kick. This is a high-scoring kick.

To close a short distance to your opponent, move your rear foot toward your front foot but don't completely close the gap between your feet. Cover only half the distance between your feet and then, with a slight jump, launch a front-foot kick.

You can also use the fast kick to avoid an attack. Follow the same technique as described earlier except move forward at a 45-degree angle to the right or left of your opponent's approach. Cross your rear foot behind your front foot for a quick change in foot position. Use your front foot for the kick. Follow up with a block and punch or kick or create an opportunity for another offensive strike.

One Step Forward

Move your weight forward as you step with your right foot and slightly pivot on your left foot (figure 5.7*a*), changing your body position from closed to open or open to closed (figure 5.7*b*). Usually the one step forward leads to a kick with

a   b

Figure 5.7   One step forward: *(a)* step with right foot and pivot on left foot; *(b)* change body position.

One step forward.

the rear leg, but it could also be used as a faking motion. If your timing is off, block your opponent's kick with one arm and punch with the other.

One step forward is usually used as an attack step to create an opportunity for a strike and to control distance. It is a good step to use with a left-foot roundhouse kick, combination double round, axe, or spin back kick.

Running (or Quick) Step

The running step is also called the quick step (figure 5.8). Where one step forward is slow, the running step is fast. Bring the rear leg forward in a running motion. Shift your front foot back about half a step. Move your body weight forward slightly and execute a rear axe, roundhouse or double roundhouse, or pushing kick as your rear leg comes forward. The quick forward action can be used to charge the opponent or close a gap. If you know your opponent is apt to retreat, you can use the running step as a fake.

a   *b*

Figure 5.8   Running step: *(a)* rear leg comes forward in a running motion; *(b)* shift weight back and execute a rear-leg kick.

Running, or quick, step.

180-Degree Forward Step (Tornado Step)

The 180-degree forward step (figure 5.9) is also known as a tornado kick or turning kick when combined with a round kick, but it also works well with axe kicks. It can be performed with or without a jump. This kick is usually used by lightweight athletes. If you are not good at this step, don't use it. The turning of the torso can add an element of surprise and may also allow you to close a gap between you and your opponent. It is a difficult kick and requires excellent balance.

a   *b*   *c*

Figure 5.9   180-degree forward step: *(a)* begin in a balanced stance; *(b)* pivot on front foot and rotate body 180 degrees, looking over your shoulder; *(c)* plant your rear foot and pivot toward opponent.

To execute the 180-degree forward step without a jump, pivot on your front foot to reverse your foot position as in a rear kick. Your feet don't move forward or backward. Slide your rear foot forward clockwise and rotate your body 180 degrees. Look over your shoulder to the target. Plant your rear foot and pivot both feet toward your opponent. Execute a rear-leg double or triple round combination.

180-degree forward step without jump.

To execute the 180-degree forward step with a jump, pivot on your front foot to reverse your foot position as in a rear kick. Execute the same motions as described previously except do not plant your rear foot after your body rotates. Slide the back foot forward in the air. Rotate your body as you keep your foot in the air as if the foot were planted on an imaginary box. Lean back slightly. With a slight jump, execute a rear-leg strike with the left leg. This move is often used when an opponent retreats or when you want to launch a surprise attack. The step works well with roundhouse kicks and even with down axe kicks and pushing kicks.

180-degree forward step with jump.

STEPS TO THE SIDE

Steps to the side can be used as part of a counterattack when an opponent is moving forward with a fast-kick, running step, or rear-leg spin back kick. It's a good way to fake the direction of your strike and to break the rhythm of an opponent's combination attack. The object is to move 45 to 90 degrees left or right in a direct sideways motion, slightly forward, or slightly back. There are five different methods.

1. Shift your body weight forward to your front foot (figure 5.10a). Step to the left in a clockwise motion with your rear (right) foot, about 45 to 90 degrees (figure 5.10b). This will shift your torso away from the oncoming kick. Set down your right foot and push off for a rear-leg kick or punch the chest and follow up with a combination double round or spin back.

2. If your opponent is attacking when your back is turned, shift your weight forward on the ball of your foot (figure 5.11a). Pivot on the ball of your front foot and sidestep to the right (counterclockwise) 45 to 90 degrees with your rear foot (figure 5.11b). Slide your left foot in the same sideways direction toward your right foot so that your body is to the right of your opponent's forward motion. Launch a rear- or front-leg kick. You can also punch the chest and follow up with a combination double round or spin back kick.

3. As you step off to the side and shift your body weight to your right leg, bend your knee in preparation for the kick. Push off the floor with your right foot. Replace your right foot with your left foot and launch the kick. A roundhouse, down axe, or crescent kick could be used. Also, when you step to the

a   *b*

Figure 5.10   Step to the side: *(a)* shift weight to front foot; *(b)* step left with rear foot.

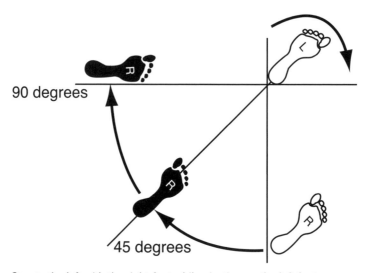

Step to the left with the right foot while pivoting on the left foot.

side, you could hint that a fake roundhouse kick might precede the side step before the kick is launched.

4. If your opponent is attacking with the front foot, slide your front (left) foot 45 degrees to the left (figure 5.12*a*) and follow with the right foot (figure 5.12*b*). Shift your body weight first to the left foot and then to the right foot

when the right foot moves in. Bend your knee and push off your leg for a left-leg kick (figure 5.12c). This is very much like the first method described except that the left leg makes the initial move and it is the left leg that kicks.

a   *b*

Figure 5.11 Step to the side: *(a)* shift weight forward; *(b)* step to the right with rear foot.

a   *b*   *c*

Figure 5.12 Step to the side: *(a)* move left foot to the left 45 degrees; *(b)* bring right foot beside it; *(c)* execute a kick with the left leg.

5. The twist step (figure 5.13) moves your body off to the side more quickly than a side step. Slide your front foot sideways in front of your body and to the inside about 45 degrees out of your opponent's line of forward motion. Replace your rear foot with your front foot. With a slight jump as your feet switch positions, simultaneously launch a rear-leg strike. This is one of the most common steps in a counterattack.

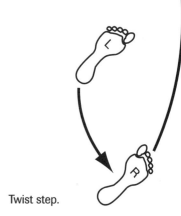

Kick

a

Twist step.

b

c

Figure 5.13   Twist step: *(a)* bring front foot sideways; *(b)* slightly jump and switch feet; *(c)* execute a rear-leg kick.

6. If your opponent is attacking with the rear foot, shift your body forward and slide your rear (right) foot 45 degrees to the right (figure 5.14*a*). Slide your front (left) foot to your right foot (figure 5.14*b*), turn your body toward the target, and launch a rear-foot kick (figure 5.14*c*).

a *b* *c*

Figure 5.14 Step to the side: *(a)* move rear foot 45 degrees to the right; *(b)* bring front foot to rear foot; *(c)* execute a rear-leg kick.

STEPS BACK

Backward steps are used mostly in counterattacks, first to avoid an attack and then to create an opening for an attack. Do not mistake this as a retreat step in response to an attacking opponent. If your reaction is late in answer to an attack, you may want to use a backward step to gain that moment of timing for a counterattack.

For backward motions, it is important to maintain balance by staying centered over your feet. Bend your knees and lower your stance as you lift your heels slightly off the floor to generate maximum acceleration. Close the gap to your opponent, using either a short or long stride.

Backward Shuffle Step

There are different ways to use shuffle steps. For the two-foot backward shuffle step, both feet move backward at the same time. Balance your weight on the balls of your feet. You can shuffle backward by stepping with the rear foot first;

the rear foot retreats and then the front foot slides backward an equal distance (figure 5.15). You can also shuffle backward by moving the front foot first; the front foot retreats and then the rear foot slides backward an equal distance.

Two-foot shuffle backward step, rear foot first.

a   *b*

Figure 5.15   Backward shuffle step, rear foot first: *(a)* rear foot moves back; *(b)* front foot moves back.

When executing a shuffle step, maintain your balance and keep your weight centered over your feet. Bend your knees and lower your stance as you lift your heels slightly off the floor. This will provide maximum flexibility. Close the gap to your opponent by using either short or long strides.

One Step Backward

When you take one step backward, you can bring the front foot straight back or move it at a 45-degree angle to either side for a rear-leg attack. You will want to use this step when the opponent is attacking with a fast kick, one step forward kick, or running step. It is very similar to the side step except the left foot goes back farther and the body position switches.

When moving straight back, take one step backward with the front foot (figure 5.16). Do not pivot on that foot; rather, place it to the rear without setting the heel down and use that same foot to push off for a kick. The foot that was used to step back is the foot used for the kick. The degree of the pivot is

a   b

Figure 5.16 One step backward: *(a)* step back with the front foot; *(b)* when bringing the foot down, do not let the heel touch down.

not important. This back step is used more often than a complete change of body position.

One step straight back.

The front one step backward at a 45-degree angle (figure 5.17) is a switch-foot step. The front foot moves back and left at a 45-degree

a   b

Figure 5.17 One step backward, 45-degree angle: *(a)* step back with the front foot; *(b)* front foot ends up at a 45-degree angle to the back foot.

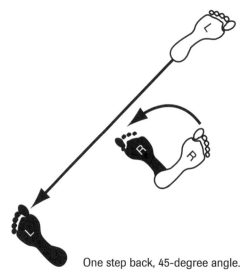

angle away from the fighters. Then the rear foot slides back to the front foot's position, and the attack is made with the left leg. If the opponent is close, it is not necessary to slide the right foot all the way back. Simply attack after bringing the front leg back. Remember to rotate the hip. The pattern of the step resembles a triangle.

One step back, 45-degree angle.

180-Degree Backward Step (Reverse Tornado Step)

The 180-degree backward step (figure 5.18) takes the inside clockwise approach. This is also known as a reverse tornado kick. The front foot moves back and you step inside or clockwise, your front foot passing in front of your rear leg as if turning your back on your opponent. Plant your left foot to the rear and then pivot both feet so your torso is turned toward your opponent. Once you are facing your opponent, execute a left roundhouse kick, crescent kick, or down axe kick. Speed is of the essence.

a   b   c

Figure 5.18 Reverse tornado: *(a)* front foot steps toward the back; *(b)* step clockwise, turning back to opponent as foot comes around; *(c)* plant left foot to the rear.

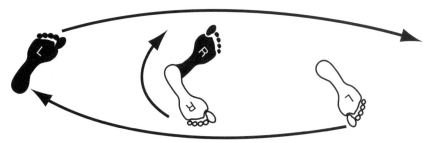

Reverse tornado kick without jump.

The tornado step can also be executed with a jump. Instead of planting the left foot to the rear, pretend you are planting it on an imaginary box. Rotate the body, keep the foot in the air, lean the upper body slightly backward, and with a slight jump, execute a rear-leg strike.

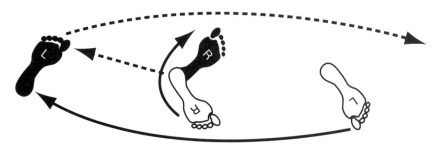

Reverse tornado kick with jump.

Fast Backward Step

The fast backward step (figure 5.19) is a reverse version of the fast-kick step (page 58). It's similar to the shuffle back step or pulling step in reverse where feet come together as opposed to remaining equidistant. Slide your front foot back to your rear foot. Move your rear foot back in a second, almost simultaneous, motion. Execute a front- or rear-leg kick.

Figure 5.19 Fast backward step: *(a)* begin to bring front foot back.

a

(continued)

b   *c*

Figure 5.19 Fast backward step *(continued): (b)* feet come together; *(c)* rear foot moves back.

Rechamber Step

If your rear-leg kick fails or if you want to execute a deliberate faking motion, drop your foot forward after the failed kick or the fake, rechamber your leg to the beginning position, and immediately spring forward with a rear-leg kick. Alternatively, you could lean back on the rechambered leg and execute a front-leg strike. The rechamber step is usually used with a right-foot roundhouse kick, axe or double roundhouse kick, or a spin hook and back kick. It is also used to back out of a clinch situation and add distance.

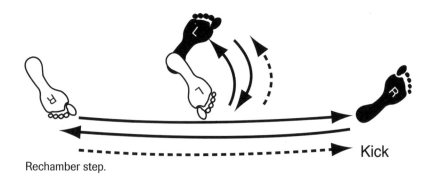

Rechamber step.

6

Taking Competitive Stances

A balanced stance is required in nearly every sport. In taekwondo, a balanced stance prepares fighters for changes in motion and gives them the flexibility to move based on the opponent's position, distance, and movement. A good stance allows fighters to maintain balance and shift their center of gravity as necessary while reacting to the opponent's moves. Training in the proper competitive stance is required to improve stability and balance.

A natural stance is a stance that fits the physical conditions of the individual fighter. It can reduce unnecessary energy consumption and fatigue. If the natural stance also enables the use of the necessary muscles only, it can ease muscular tension and expedite the exercise.

For a good stance, you must have harmony between muscular power and flexibility. The proper stance enables you to use your flexibility to support your body weight while standing or moving. Quickly shift your center of gravity by moving one or both feet while making dodging motions to the front, side, or back. After attack and counterattack, maintain your balance by bending your knees 45 to 110 degrees.

You can increase stability by broadening the base of support. A narrow base of support increases speed for attack or counterattack, but it also makes it difficult to generate strong kicks and score high marks. If you spread your feet too far apart, you will have better stability but the width of the stance may hamper your ability to move.

Taekwondo kicks and punches are performed at various axes of the joints. The positions and angles of the feet vary depending on the physical condition of the athlete and the athlete's style of attack and defense. The stances covered in this chapter provide the foundation for all of the kicks, punches, and blocks performed by taekwondo fighters. The stance is a critical element of taekwondo. Practice your stances often, and practice in front of a mirror when you can.

EVALUATING SPARRING STANCES

The sparring stance is a basic element for attack and defense. The sparring stance is an important aspect of an athlete's contest style, whether attacking or defending. Learn to read your opponents' stances in order to determine the type of fighter they are. Recognizing certain styles will prepare you to defend against particular attacks.

a

In the ring, stances are classified as closed or open to define how opponents relate to each other by position. When both contestants are facing each other and have the same foot position, they are both in a closed stance (figure 6.1*a*). In a closed stance, your feet are in the same position as your opponent's. For example, if your opponent's right foot is to the front as you face each other, your right foot is to the front.

When both contestants are looking in the same direction, they are in an open stance (figure 6.1*b*). Your feet are in a position that mirrors your opponent's feet. For example, if your opponent's right foot is to the front, your left foot is to the front.

b

Figure 6.1   Stances: *(a)* closed stance; *(b)* open stance.

USING SPARRING STANCES

The three sparring stances are the basic attack sparring stance, the sideways sparring stance, and the neutral sparring stance. In each case, the distance between the feet is important. Spread your feet shoulder-width apart or slightly wider. When you take a stable stance with knees bent and a lower center of gravity, you can feel the increase in stability. A broad base of support makes it easy to maintain stability on the ground. A high level of stability may cause a decrease in speed, but you should still be able to execute a strong, long kick.

Basic Attack Sparring Stance

In the basic attack sparring stance (figure 6.2), the center of gravity is between the feet and legs. The front and back feet are placed at the same angle and face front. The attack stance enables the use of one foot at the front and one foot at the back or the use of both feet. It works well for dealing with an attacking opponent.

Slightly lift your heels to give yourself a chance to move quickly. Keep the knees flexed in order to quickly initiate skills such as snap kicks, round kicks, down axe kicks, punches, and front counterkicks.

Figure 6.2 Basic attack sparring stance.

The weakness of the basic attack sparring stance is that it is difficult to generate speed for turning kicks such as spin back kicks and spin hook kicks since the torso is mostly facing the opponent and therefore requires a full turning radius.

Neutral Sparring Stance

In the neutral stance (figure 6.3), the feet are at a right angle to each other, angling the torso slightly away from facing front. The foot placement of the neutral stance is in between that of the attack stance and the sideways stance,

Figure 6.3   Neutral sparring stance.

thus allowing for an excellent range of offensive and defensive kicks. Since the body is not turned directly forward, the opportunity for front, side, and spin kicks is maximized. Whereas the sideways stance is better for spin or side kicks and the attack stance is better for front- or rear-leg kicks, the neutral stance is somewhere in between. Also, since the body is slightly turned away from the front, when a kick is launched and there is twisting at the waist, the force of mass with speed produces more power in the attack.

Sideways Sparring Stance

The sideways sparring stance (figure 6.4) enables flexibility for side kicks, sliding and pulling steps, front-leg kicks, offensive and defensive spin back kicks, and spin hook kicks. However, this stance will slow down a back round kick since the torso is turned slightly away from a directly forward angle. Both feet are at the same angle and are perpendicular to the opponent.

Figure 6.4   Sideways sparring stance.

7

Using Feints and Timing

Feinting motions are a strategy for deceiving opponents. The purpose of feints, or fakes, is to secure the upper hand in the match by hiding your real attack strategy and confusing your opponent. Feints are nothing more than initiations of skill sets that are not fully executed. You can build a feint from any step, kick, or footwork.

This chapter covers the concept of feints and timing, important skills to incorporate into your strategy in the ring. All chapters that discuss training drills, attacks, counterattacks, and footwork also include feints and timing.

FEINTING

Although feints are not unique to taekwondo, each sport has specific body movements for feinting. In basketball and American football, for example, players may fake a pass or shot to mislead their opponents and force their opponents to change speed or direction. In judo or wrestling, fighters often use a grappling movement as a fake. Those moves are specific to those sports. In taekwondo, the feint is used to "fish" or elicit a response from the opponent. If the feint is successful, it creates an opportunity for the athlete to score by throwing the opponent off balance and exposing a weakness.

Taekwondo attacks can be direct or indirect. In a direct attack, the fighter comes straight in for a point. In an indirect attack, the fighter uses a feint or a step before the attack. If you have the chance to score easily through a preemptive attack, that is the best way to win a match. Both direct and indirect attacks include an advancing motion.

Feinting does carry risks. An ill-timed or poorly executed feint may expose a weakness to your opponent. Remember, your opponent is also waiting for a chance to attack. As you try to figure out your opponent's next move, remain on guard for a surprise attack from your opponent.

You can use feinting to create an attacking opportunity by exposing a weakness to your opponent in order to draw an attack, allowing you to counterattack. A good feint might also expose a weakness of your opponent.

As in other sports, in taekwondo feinting is used to make the game more interesting, to gain an advantage over an opponent, to expose any weaknesses of an opponent, or to make an opponent guess the direction of your attack.

A preemptive attack of more than two motions—a feint and footwork, footwork and kick or punch, and so on—has a higher rate of success than a multiple counter, single counter, or single direct attack. The high success rate of a multiskill attack that includes feinting demonstrates the importance of feinting skill.

Various kinds of feint motions are as follows:

- Use upper-body motion. Slightly dip your trunk forward and then return to your original position.
- Begin a feinting attack by sliding your front foot forward. Sell the feint with your entire body, including your eyes, shoulders, hands, arms, and feet. Return to your original position.
- Advance one step and then step to the side with the same foot and pivot.
- Advance with short running (quick) steps.
- Change your stance from open to closed or closed to open.
- Execute a low cut kick with your left or right foot.
- Advance one step with your back foot, then shuffle back two steps or retreat 45 degrees to the side.
- Feint an attack with your back foot as if you were going to kick, but instead set it down next to your front foot. With your front foot, retreat back or at a 45-degree angle.
- Slide the rear foot to the front and use the front foot for a short, low cut kick, then return to your stance.
- Take one step forward in a rear-foot kicking motion, but instead plant your foot and then bound back to your original position.
- Turn your torso as if to start a spin kick but quickly return to a forward stance for an attack such as a spin back kick, tornado kick, back kick, or spin hook kick.

Other skills such as changing stances, twisting, skipping, jumping, turning, and clinching can be used as feints.

Excellent athletes prepare their attack and defense motions in advance by predicting the opponent's next move. Recognize the feinting motions your opponent uses; this will help you see your opponent's weaknesses and will prompt certain attacks. Practice feinting moves in front of a mirror and try different kinds of feints with different opponents in order to improve your ability to predict your opponent's reactions to your moves.

TIMING

A good sparring stance allows you to instantly adjust your kicks when your opponent changes motions. Making adjustments with good timing is a key to success in competitive taekwondo.

Timing can be classified into three types: preemptive attack, simultaneous attack, and dodge and counterattack. (Refer to chapters 10 and 11 for more detailed information.) Good timing provides the best chance for an attack and has a higher rate of success. A fighter with poor timing will have ineffective motions and will fail to respond with timely skills against the opponent. Speed is a vital part of timing, enabling successful attacks.

For example, both fighters are in a sparring stance. Fighter A moves the right foot in order to attempt a double round kick. Before fighter A makes a second motion with the left foot, fighter B executes a jump back kick from a stationary position. If the moment is lost for fighter B as fighter A moves in with the double, then another opportunity comes by shuffling back to avoid the kick, waiting for fighter A to drop the kick forward, then attacking. Athletes who

A fighter with good timing is able to dodge and counterattack with speed and power.

are unable to capitalize on these brief windows of opportunity are unable to get high scores and also expose themselves to attacks.

Good timing allows athletes to use their skills confidently and successfully through preemptive attacks. They can influence their opponent's reaction and take advantage when the opponent makes an improper body motion, changes stance, hesitates, shows evidence of overexertion or fatigue, or moves backward frequently. A preemptive strategy is born of courage, ability to make fast decisions, speed, and an absolute trust in ability. It's not necessarily wise to come out kicking after the referee initiates the fight. It is important to "check" first and feint to get a good read of the opponent. If the opponent is a good counterattacker, then preemptive attacks may be poor strategy.

The best time for a simultaneous counterattack is when your opponent attacks or is induced to attack through a feint. By using the opponent's forward momentum, you can increase the impact of the counterattack. With solid technique and blocking in a simultaneous attack, you can produce a scoring kick. Often both athletes attack with the same kick. Based on your specialty, there may be times when giving up a point will garner 2 points by way of a head shot or knockdown. For example, in a simultaneous attack, fighter A launches a solid round kick and scores. But fighter B was coming in with an axe kick and makes contact on the face—2 points against 1 point. If fighter B's block of the round kick was good, then a solid 2 points have been scored. It can boil down to not being afraid to get hit.

Dodging and counterattacking is a good way to carry out a planned attack. Move back to escape your opponent's attack and grasp the opportune moment to counter when your opponent's feet are in the air or just as the feet touch the ground, or when the opponent falls off balance. This method may be necessary if the opponent is faster than you. Using proper timing and controlling distance are integral to this method. Fishing for a response and watching for vulnerable moments can give a slower fighter a strong counterstrategy. This method is also good for fighting against someone who has an attacking style and is always coming at you. You can move sideways and counter with a kick. The opportunity to attack comes when your opponent's attack is ending.

To catch the window of opportunity, you must intuitively sense your opponent's movement. Depending on your opponent's movement, reflectively react with your eyes and body. Timing means responding with the proper skill at the right speed at the right time. This kind of reaction can be improved through repetitive training.

In competition, the preferred preemptive attack skills are round kick to trunk, back kick to trunk, pushing kick to trunk, down axe kick to face, round kick to face, front hook kick to face, and spin hook kick to face.

The first and second attacks are planned before the match. However, excellent fighters should be able to attack and counterattack continuously, depending on the opponent's movements. Athletes who have trained repetitively will be able to make automatic adjustments in the fleeting moment they have to react.

8

Developing the Mind of a Champion

Successful athletes are confident. They are able to control their anxiety, concentrate under distracting conditions, and visualize victory. Confidence leads to success because it provides a foundation for psychological stability. Mental toughness on top of physical strength and honed skills is a potent combination.

Confidence works together with concentration to enable the athlete to carry out strategies. A confident athlete is able to make proper judgments during a match. When confidence is low, concentration is also affected. An athlete who fears injury or failure will not perform well during the match.

Confidence and concentration make it easier for an athlete to exercise self-control and relax, even under the pressure of competition. This attitude is linked to a dauntless spirit, a desire for victory, and a love of adventure, all of which lead to competitive success.

Confidence induces an athlete to set challenging goals. Through ambitious goals, athletes are inspired to exert themselves toward more progressive efforts. On the other hand, athletes who lack self-confidence have difficulty setting goals, which hinders their progress.

Imagery, or visualization, has been used for mental training, mental recollection, and psychological therapy. Athletes frequently use imagery as a form of mental training to improve performance. Visualization can be done before, during, or after a match or during rest. This mental preparedness can help to relieve event anxiety. If the physical aspect of preparation has been carefully planned and executed, then the mental aspect completes the cycle and elicits a feeling of organization and thoroughness.

Imagery is based on experience and imagination rather than physical exercise. You can mentally relive your own past matches, watch videotapes of past matches or of certain athletes, or envision positive outcomes for events to come.

When all is said and done, sometimes it is the spirit of the soul that engenders the confidence and mental toughness necessary to win. For example, let's say two athletes have been injured during a match round, have tied scores in their respective matches, and now must decide to continue or discontinue. The weaker of the two in mind and spirit will quit the match. The other will persevere and take a chance, maybe even win.

It is this spirit that was evident in the World Junior Taekwondo Championship some years back. An athlete I coached was injured in the semifinal rounds. Winning would take him to the Junior Olympics; losing would be the end of the line for him. But to give up without trying would seal his fate without question. He decided to take his chances even though doctors recommended that he stop. He had come this far and had a strong desire to win. With a specific coaching strategy from me that took into account his injured foot, he was able to win his match in the third round. He went on to compete in the Junior Olympics.

An athlete who has a low physical threshold of capability must overcome that limitation by having a willing spirit. If the spirit is not willing, then she cannot surpass her physical limits. It is also true that if the body is able but the spirit is not willing, then the athlete cannot move forward. She must use the spirit to nourish the physical and use the physical to build the confidence of the spirit. It is important to build endurance by overcoming spiritual and physical limits. Each time a threshold of capability is surpassed, the spirit is fed and the body increases its fitness.

CONFIDENCE

Confidence can be defined as the conviction that success will come. Confident athletes are sure of a successful performance in an upcoming match and are able to objectively grasp the situation and cope with it. Athletes who lack self-assurance will have difficulty performing because of psychological anxiety and fear before the match. Self-assurance is a decisive psychological element of a successful competitive performance.

The key to generating the maximum level of skill in a match is a proper level of confidence. Overconfidence or underconfidence will lead to diminished performance.

I have taught students who could use their skill and knowledge fully during practice but performed poorly in real matches. They didn't live up to their potential because of their lack of confidence. Their anxiety before the match

A fighter with the right level of confidence enters the arena with the mental advantage.

created tension. Their distrust of their own skills heightened the tension, interfering with their concentration. Their fear of failure and inability to concentrate because of that fear led to real failure, which further diminished their confidence.

I recall a student of mine, a national competitor, who was nervous about an upcoming event. This young man was a rising star. He had great skills but lacked a little in confidence. I arranged for him to spar with a U.S. national team member and World Cup gold medalist. I told the rising star all about the U.S. team member, and he got very nervous about the match. However, behind the scenes I asked the U.S. team member to take it easy on the young man and exercise control. Of course, the rising star didn't know about my conversation and I told him to give it his best shot—maybe he could win. The rising star did win the match and his confidence shot up like a rocket. His bravery increased tenfold and he went on to win many matches.

Athletes who are overconfident may have the same kinds of experiences as athletes who lack confidence. Overconfident athletes overestimate their abilities and fail to concentrate during the match. They are easily agitated, which leads to anxiety and tension. Often they expose their weaknesses to the opponent by attempting unreasonable attacks. Overconfidence may cause athletes to neglect their training in preparation for the match. They may be distracted by the competitive environment and lack internal psychological control.

Confidence can be developed to the proper level. Successful past experiences can be connected to confident thoughts and actions. To develop confidence, an athlete needs to work through each of the following steps:

- Sufficient training—Train in an environment that simulates match conditions as much as possible.

- Ample match experience—Gain experience in local matches in which winning or losing is not as important as in a major event.

- Acquisition of new skills—Practice new skills until they become second nature, keeping in mind what techniques are restricted in a match.

- Feedback from coaches and colleagues—Evaluate strengths and shortcomings during training and after each match.

- Confident actions and thoughts—Stop thinking about your opponent's skill and don't dwell on fears of getting hurt during a match.

- Imagery—Imagine success in critical match situations against a virtual opponent.

Confidence is fostered when athletes visualize themselves overcoming difficult situations from the past. Athletes can draw up a blueprint for success in future matches based on experiences of past matches.

Practice and experience in various matches play a decisive role in boosting confidence. To build confidence, continue to improve certain skills and cultivate positive thinking about winning. Foster a can-do spirit. You will be able to concentrate on the match if you are confident in your ability to launch a successful attack.

CONTROL

Athletes in individual sports such as taekwondo, boxing, and wrestling are more prone to psychological stress and anxiety than athletes in team sports. Tension and anxiety are psychological states created by internal and external stimuli. Psychological pressure and a lack of confidence add to tension and lead to unpredictable results. This tension reaches its peak when names are called and matches begin. Excellent athletes have the ability to overcome tension and anxiety and find serenity, even in pressure-packed competitive situations.

Tension and anxiety are demonstrated in physical, psychological, and behavioral ways. Physiologically, tension might increase the heart rate, raise blood pressure, produce sweaty feet and hands, create a strong need to urinate, or make the muscles more rigid. These physical symptoms of anxiety can dull speed and balance. Psychological reactions to tension include anxiety, uneasiness, confusion, lack of concentration, lack of self-confidence, loss of desire, and excessive fear. Behavioral reactions include fidgeting, confusion, lack of concentration, and anxiety.

Anxiety can affect even well-trained athletes. Athletes who are expected to do well in a match because of excellent performance in practice matches and high level of skill may then perform inadequately in a real match. When athletes fail by a slight difference in scores, their motivation may increase with the anticipation that they might perform better next time. On the other hand, their motivation may decline. In any case, their failure in the competitive environment was most likely due to their failure to overcome anxiety.

I can't stress enough the importance of training in real matches. The experience of one-on-one sparring can help you build your repertoire of strategies. For example, sometimes in national and international events, a lottery is used to determine which teams fight and in what order. The U.S. team did not want to face the team to beat early in the event and possibly face immediate elimination. By avoiding the premier team, perhaps they could at least get to the semifinals. This fear of the other team was a problem. The remedy was to bring several teams together, including the top adversary, at a camp twice a year and practice in a noncompetitive atmosphere. The change of venue alleviated the fears of the U.S. team and leveled the emotional playing ground for the international competition.

Tension and anxiety aren't always negative, however. A proper level of tension and anxiety heightens mental concentration and, as such, is a positive element.

Athletes should learn to control their anxiety by analyzing the source of that anxiety and understanding its physical effects in order to maintain the proper level of tension for the match. In doing so, the athletes will be able to overcome psychological pressure before and during the match. Watch for these factors as they can affect the performance of taekwondo athletes:

- Fear of failing to live up to the expectations of other people
- Lack of physical and psychological preparation (lack of exercise, past injury, failure at new skills and strategy)
- Unfamiliar and chaotic match site (large crowd, high-stakes match, opponent's reputation)
- Unfair decisions by the judge

New athletes and those with little competitive experience struggle with tension and anxiety more frequently than seasoned competitors. Such tension and anxiety may disrupt mental concentration, which, in turn, can limit success in a match. Learning to resolve tension and anxiety by analyzing the cause is important.

There are both physical and psychological methods for controlling anxiety. Relieving tension physically involves breath control and muscle relaxation. Breath control is an excellent technique for controlling tension and anxiety. Through breath control, athletes feel a natural reduction of tension and anxiety. Flexibility is also increased due to the relaxation of the autonomic nervous system.

Stand or sit on the floor or a bench with your legs comfortably crossed. Flatten both hands on your stomach under your navel. Slowly bend forward at the waist. Pull your abdomen toward your back and count to 10 as you exhale all the air from your lungs as if you were releasing air from a balloon. Hold the exhalation for a count of 5. Slowly raise your shoulders up (standing or sitting), then count to 10 and inhale through your nose. For another count of 5, exhale through pursed lips. Concentrate on the sound of the air filling your lungs as it is expelled. Listen to the resonance in your head and shut out any external distractions. Clear your mind of the match and concentrate on slowing down. You should feel your abdomen distend in order to expand the lungs and take in more air; simply raising the shoulders does not accomplish a full intake of air. Repeat the cycle slowly five or six times. You should be able to slow your heart rate and relax.

Relaxation that targets specific muscles can be used to relieve the muscular rigidity that results from tension. This technique requires the tightening and relaxing of an area of the body—arm, calf, thigh, neck, and so on—that may be tense. Select a problem area, the biceps for example, and flex the muscle to the count of 10. Slowly relax the muscle. Do this several times until the muscle feels relaxed.

Mental relaxation is as important as physical relaxation for relieving anxiety. Negative self-talk only elevates tension and anxiety. Wipe your mind clean of negative experiences and undesirable thoughts about the upcoming match. Think back to successful situations and the positive results of dedicated practice. Turn self-talk into a positive mantra, such as "I can do this." Repeat this thought while envisioning techniques for a successful match.

CONCENTRATION

Concentration is a psychological technique that can be mastered with practice. As in any sport, taekwondo athletes must rely on more than just physical preparation. Focus plays a vital role in any sport in which competition is one on one or in which athletes compete as individuals. For example, an archer must focus completely on the target before releasing the arrow. All phases of concentration and physical ability have to synchronize for the arrow to meet the target.

Mental concentration is crucial for advancement in a sport. Focus is an expression of mental ability and the desire to accomplish goals, backed up by an appetite for winning matches. Concentration in a match separates the winners from the losers.

The nature of a taekwondo match demands use of maximum skill and concentration. An athlete who can concentrate will be able to respond quickly to the moves of the opponent. She must focus on the actions and intentions of the opponent and changes in the match situation, quickly process it all, and respond for a score.

In addition to concentrating on timing and individual match situations, athletes always need to concentrate on the entire game. It is necessary to overcome any elements that interfere with concentration, such as the following:

- Lack of preparation due to overconfidence
- Excessive anxiety and fear of failure due to lack of confidence
- Dwelling on past match failures, injuries, or unfair decisions by a judge
- Match situations such as being scored on, making a score, or having the match interrupted due to injury
- External factors such as weather conditions, a new environment, and the presence of spectators

Athletes should be trained to concentrate under any circumstances. Concentration comes from practice, practice, practice. Partner drills, paddle drills, and ho gu drills, as explained in chapter 9, focus on target accuracy, timing, and speed. The action of linking basic skills in a sequence requires concentration to coordinate the body's movements. For beginners, a simple sequence such as a low block, punch, and step forward can be difficult to execute. The body learns and the muscles begin to develop memory after repetitive actions. The synchronization of mind and muscle comes from practice.

Anything that might cause excessive tension or anxiety should be planned for in advance. Consider the patience demonstrated by marathon runners. As with marathon runners, successful taekwondo athletes display a strong desire to win by overcoming physical and psychological pain through self-control. The proper level of tension and focus is required moment by moment. You must ignore elements not directly related to the match and concentrate only on the essential aspects.

VISUALIZATION

Actors memorize a script so they can recapture in their mind the scenes required for a role. In the same way, athletes can mentally experience a successful match well in advance of the actual match.

Athletes with more experience and skill enjoy greater success with imagery than athletes with little experience from which to draw. Athletes who train diligently and compete regularly in local matches are better equipped psychologically and physically to compete in the matches that count.

When mentally training for a specific match, you need to know certain information, such as the size of the competition, the location, the competitors, and the time of the match. Once you have this information, imagery can be included as part of your psychological preparation.

During visualization, you experience the style of an opponent by mentally participating in the match. Mentally prepare to react to different styles of attack and defense, prepare for counterattacks and defense, or think about what to do when you are close to losing the match and there are only 30 seconds left. Recapture the situation in your mind and work through it. This forethought and familiarization will prepare you to control the situation in a real match. Improving your ability to cope with difficult situations will help you relax and heighten your concentration. The mental transfer of skills in visualization builds confidence and enables correct judgment in difficult situations.

There are many imagery techniques. Which method you use depends on the information and equipment at your disposal, your personality, and the strength of your imagination. Choose the method that suits you best.

- Watch videotapes or films of sanctioned domestic or international matches. Watching top athletes at work is a great way to increase motivation. Analyze their attack and defense styles and the variety of attack and defense situations they face. This will help you cope with your own shortcomings and improve your strengths. Make mental notes of important scenes and recapture various situations as if they were your own experiences.

- Recall your own match experiences. When recalling a match, factor in training drills and exercise. Analyze what worked in the match and what didn't. Adjust your training schedule accordingly to overcome weaknesses and improve your ability to cope with difficult situations.

- When the date of the match is set, imagine situations that might create psychological stress. For example, imagine bad weather conditions, an unfamiliar and chaotic match site with many spectators, injuries, or unknown opponents. What methods can you use to cope with the offensive and defensive styles of the different athletes? What will you do if you are driven into a corner? How will you handle a slight difference in scores? You will improve your mental toughness by repeatedly imagining difficult situations and coping with those situations mentally in advance of the match.

- Use your imagination. After watching a movie, do scenes remain in your mind because of a personal connection? Apply this experience to mental training in taekwondo. As you watch tapes of other athletes, choose an athlete and imagine yourself as the opponent of that athlete. Make it personal. Close your eyes and engage in the match. Imagine a situation in which an athlete sizes up an opponent correctly and wins the match after a vigorous and skillful contest. Highlight the important moves and memorize them. Free imagery makes it possible for you to practice new skills and tactics as though participating in a real match. This psychological skill of transference helps to develop coping and adaptation skills.

9

Drilling for Competition

Competition is the culmination of training and sparring, linking basic techniques and professional training to success in the ring. Statistically, round kicks, axe kicks, back kicks, and punch combinations score more points in the ring; therefore, in this chapter we focus on drills for these techniques.

Training has many levels. Students can train alone in front of a mirror or with equipment, and they can train with partners or in groups. Training in simulation sparring is especially important for gaining experience in the competitive arena. Knowing what technique works best for you will help you plan a strategy for competitions. A particular technique may become a specialty of yours in the ring.

It is necessary to train with sparring partners with different levels of skill and strategy, which will help build confidence. Remember, it is not important whether you win or lose; it is important that you gain experience. Participate in local events whenever possible. You may be a star in your own school, but you may not measure up outside of that environment. To be ready for what an opponent may throw at you means doing time at smaller events.

This chapter covers a variety of training drills including attacks and counterattacks, step techniques, knee kicks, running kicks, and target skills. These drills are just suggestions to help you get started. I have used all of them at one time or another in my own dojang and with national teams. Good training builds endurance, physical strength, speed, and agility. These traits in turn form a strong base for building confidence.

ATTACK DRILLS

The focus of attack drills is the forward motion of the athlete. You want to be able to execute all kicks from a stationary position, but you also need to execute those kicks while closing a gap or using offensive strategy in a match. Balance and strength are required to keep the forward momentum, make the strike, and maintain an upright position at the end of it all. The following exercises build from the in-place position and incorporate steps in combination with basic kicks.

Basic Kicks With Mirror

The training focus for this drill is correct technique, posture, and accuracy.

Drill 1   Execute front kicks to the trunk or face.

Drill 2   Execute round kicks to the trunk or face.

Drill 3   Execute front hook kicks to the face.

Drill 4   Execute spin back kicks to the trunk or face.

Drill 5   Execute spin hook kicks to the face.

Drill 6   Execute axe kicks to the face.

Drill 7   Execute cutting or pushing kicks to the trunk.

Line up in front of a mirror, standing in ready kicking position. Execute the kick and evaluate your hip rotation and posture. Look at your shoulders, stance, leg position, and balance. If possible, have your coach evaluate your technique as well. After you execute the kick, drop your foot forward and rechamber your leg, continuing to face the mirror.

Basic Kicks With Partner

This drill can be performed by two athletes facing each other or in a group setting. The training focus is target accuracy, proper technique, and distance control.

Drill 1   Execute front kicks to the trunk or face.

Drill 2   Execute round kicks to the trunk or face (figure 9.1).

Drill 3   Execute front hook kicks to the face.

Drill 4   Execute spin back kicks to the trunk or face.

Drill 5   Execute spin hook kicks to the face.

Figure 9.1 Face partner and execute a round kick to his trunk.

Drill 6 Execute axe kicks to the face.

Drill 7 Execute cutting or pushing kicks to the trunk.

The instructor designates the kick to be used and the target area. Face your partner and take turns kicking at each other according to instructions. Focus on your target and deliver a kick at normal speed. The kick should be perfect in execution, direction, and accuracy. Look at the target and bring the kick to the exact point where you are looking. Your kicking foot should overlap the target in your line of sight. As quickly as possible, rechamber your foot for the next kick. If you are in a group setting, rotate the line so that everyone practices with everyone else.

Basic Attack With Forward Steps

This drill focuses on perfecting back-and-forth movement, weight shifts, quickness, balance, and feinting.

Drill 1 Bounce in place and execute a rear round knee kick. Drop the foot forward and turn.

Drill 2 Switch step and change stance. Execute a knee kick and reverse direction.

Drill 3 Shuffle forward. You can shuffle with the front foot first and rear foot following, with the rear foot first and then the front foot, or with both feet at the same time.

Drill 4 Execute a pulling (fast) step. Pull your rear foot to your front foot and then move your front foot forward.

Drill 5 Take one step forward.

Drill 6 Execute a running forward step. The front foot slides back slightly and the rear foot moves forward a short distance.

Drill 7 Turn back clockwise 180 degrees and execute a forward step (tornado). Pivot on the ball of the front foot.

If you are in a class with other students, line up side by side, facing the same direction. Choose which footwork pattern you will use (or listen for instructions from your instructor) and perform the steps in sets of 10. Step forward twice, reverse direction, and step forward twice again. Repeat. After completing one set of a step sequence, continue with the other training steps in sets of 10.

Focus on maintaining flexibility in the knees and performing a proper weight shift backward and forward. Be aware of your balance and practice feinting motions with your entire body. Stay relaxed as you practice and work on increasing speed and flexibility to produce fast footwork.

Step Knee Kicks (Round Kicks)

Knee kicks are a good way to practice the basic body position and motion of a technique without fully extending the leg. For a round knee kick, balance on the supporting foot. Shift your body weight and rotate the hip, lifting the knee but not extending the leg. This same method can be used with spin back kicks, pushing kicks, axe kicks, side kicks, and so on.

The focus of this drill is kicking posture, weight shifts, balance, and quickness while moving back and forth and switching directions.

Drill 1 Bounce in place and execute a rear-knee round kick. Drop your foot forward and turn.

Drill 2 Perform a switch-foot step and a rear-knee round kick. Move back and forth.

Drill 3 Execute a shuffle step, adding a rear-knee round kick. Move back and forth.

Drill 4 Perform a pulling (fast) step with a front-knee round kick. Move back and forth.

Drill 5 Take one step forward and perform a rear-knee round kick. Move back and forth.

Drill 6 Execute a running step and a rear-knee round kick. Move back and forth.

Drill 7   Turn 180 degrees and step (tornado). The rear foot turns clockwise 180 degrees. Add a rear-knee round kick.

Stand in front of a mirror if you are practicing by yourself. If you are in a group, line up side by side, everyone facing the same direction. Begin by bouncing in place with a feint. Choose which footwork pattern you will use (or listen for instructions from your coach) and perform the steps in sets of 10. Step, kick, drop kick forward (twice) then turn, changing direction, and step, kick, drop kick forward (twice), turn, and repeat. After completing one set of a particular step sequence, continue with the additional training steps in sets of 10.

Pay attention to flexibility, balance, quickness, and footwork.

Step Round Knee Kicks or Round Kicks With Partner

This drill uses the round knee kick described in the previous drill. Since there is a partner, the drill focuses on target accuracy and quick weight shifts while maintaining balance and controlling distance.

Drill 1   Bounce in place and execute a rear-knee round kick. Drop your foot forward and then back to the original position.

Drill 2   Switch your feet and execute a rear-knee round kick. Drop your foot forward after the kick and then back to the original position.

Drill 3   Shuffle forward and execute a rear-knee round kick. Drop your foot forward after the kick and then back to the original position.

Drill 4   Perform a pulling (fast) step and then a front-knee round kick. Drop your foot forward after the kick and then back to the original position.

Drill 5   Take one step forward and execute a rear-knee round kick. Drop your foot forward after the kick and then back to the original position.

Drill 6   Perform a running step and execute a rear-knee round kick. Drop your foot forward after the kick and then back to the original position.

Drill 7   Turn 180 degrees and step (tornado). The rear foot turns clockwise 180 degrees. Add a rear-knee round kick. Drop your foot forward after the kick and back to the original position.

Drill 8   Perform a cut step or pushing step (front or rear) and combine it with a coordinating round kick (front cut and left rear round right or rear cut and right rear round left). Drop your foot forward after the kick and then quickly back to the original position.

Drill 9   Hop one step and execute a rear axe kick. Drop your foot forward after the kick and then quickly return it to the original position.

Face your partner in a closed sparring stance. Begin with the first footwork pattern. Direct the kick at your partner, and then have your partner perform the drill. Using the second footwork pattern, repeat the drill. Shuffle back to your closed sparring stance after each kick. After executing the kick, quickly rechamber your leg and shuffle backward or step across to the rear. Practice accurately targeting your partner's trunk or face.

The focus of this drill is target accuracy. Even though this is a noncontact drill, distance control, balance, weight shifts, and flexibility all come into play.

Paddle Kicks With Partner

For this drill, you will need a partner who is holding two paddles. The training focus of this drill is target accuracy, contact power, follow-through, distance control, and gross motor coordination. This drill can incorporate other kicks such as the axe kick, pushing kick, back kick, or spin hook kick.

Drill 1   Bounce in place and execute a rear round kick.

Drill 2   Switch your feet and execute a rear round kick.

Drill 3   Shuffle forward and execute a rear round kick.

Drill 4   Perform a pulling (fast) step forward and execute a round kick.

Drill 5   Take one step forward and execute a rear round kick.

Drill 6   Perform a running step and execute a rear round kick.

Drill 7   Turn your rear foot 180 degrees clockwise, take a forward step, and execute a rear round kick.

Drill 8   Take a cut step or pushing step and execute a rear round kick.

Drill 9   Hop one step forward and execute a rear axe kick.

Each pattern can be done in sets of 10 or timed at 60-second intervals. Face your partner in closed sparring stance. Your partner holds the paddles. From a relaxed position, your partner moves a paddle to a position for you to kick by thrusting it forward quickly to achieve an element of surprise. This will help you develop speed, timing, and target recognition. Execute any of the step–kick drill patterns, being careful to return to your original position either by shuffling back or stepping across to the rear. Take turns executing the drills with your partner.

Chest-Pad Kicks (Ho Gu)

For this drill, you and your partner will both need a body shield or a chest pad (ho gu) with two paddles underneath for added padding (figure 9.2).

The focus is target accuracy, but this drill also helps you learn to feel the power of contact. Work on your follow-through, distance control, gross motor coordination, balance, weight shifts, and footwork. Additional kicks, such as axe kicks, pushing kicks, jump spin back kicks, spin hook kicks, or tornado kicks, could be incorporated into the drill.

Drill 1 Bounce in place and execute a rear round kick.

Drill 2 Switch your feet and stance and execute a rear round kick.

Drill 3 Shuffle forward and execute a rear round kick.

Figure 9.2 When performing chest pad kicks, you and your partner need to wear the correct safety equipment, including helmets and chest pads.

Drill 4 Perform a pulling (fast) step forward and execute a round kick.

Drill 5 Take one step forward and execute a rear round kick.

Drill 6 Perform a running step and execute a rear round kick.

Drill 7 Turn your rear foot 180 degrees clockwise, take a step forward, and execute a rear round kick.

Drill 8 Take a cut step or pushing step and execute a rear round kick (front or rear cut with coordinating round kick).

Drill 9 Hop one step forward and execute a rear axe kick.

Each pattern can be done in sets of 10 or timed at 60-second intervals. Face your partner in closed sparring stance. Both of you should wear a body shield or a chest pad with two paddles underneath. As you execute the step–kick drill patterns, be careful to maintain good distance and rechamber your leg back to its original position either by shuffling back or stepping across to the rear. You and your partner should take turns executing the drill. This drill will help both of you experience the sensation of contact and use that knowledge to develop better footwork, balance, speed, and power.

Kicking Bag

For this drill, you will need a swinging kicking bag or a floor kicking bag. In this exercise, you will feel the delivery of power in each kick and learn how each kick makes contact. Other kicks—pushing kicks, jump spin back kicks, spin hook kicks, tornado kicks—and punches could be incorporated into the drill.

Drill 1   Bounce in place and execute a rear round kick.

Drill 2   Switch feet and execute a rear round kick.

Drill 3   Perform a shuffle step and execute a rear round kick.

Drill 4   Perform a pulling (fast) step to the front and execute a rear round kick.

Drill 5   Take one step forward and execute a rear round kick.

Drill 6   Take a running step and execute a rear round kick.

Drill 7   Turn your rear foot 180 degrees forward, step, and execute a rear round kick.

Drill 8   Perform a cut step and execute a rear round kick.

Drill 9   Slide forward or to the side and execute a low block and punch.

Line up behind the kicking bag in a ready stance. Execute the kick, drop your leg forward, and quickly rechamber your leg to its original position. If multiple students are using one kicking bag, take your turn and return to the end of the line. Pay close attention to the technical delivery of each kick and step. Be aware of the power of your kick as it contacts the bag.

If you are ready for another kick, try this variation with a swinging bag. Push the bag forward, and when it swings back execute a jump spin back kick or spin hook kick. The point is to time your kick with the forward motion of the bag. This will help you learn to accurately time your kick with your opponent's forward motion.

COUNTERKICK DRILLS

The focus of these drills is to establish reactive moves to your opponent's forward motion with appropriate counterkicks and moves. There are several avenues of practice including retreating shuffle steps, side steps, knee round kicks with several different steps, drills with a partner, and drills using equipment such as paddles and kicking bags. The following drills should give you an idea of how to practice counterattack steps and kicks. Any variety of combinations can be used.

Backward Steps

Shifting your weight is important when moving backward. Even though the movement is backward, the weight is mostly forward. The weight shifts momentarily to the back foot during movement but ultimately is centered over the front foot. Shift your weight back and forth after any back step in order to be ready for kicking. Practice once or twice backward, then turn and reverse directions, repeating the backward motion of each step.

Drill 1   Execute a shuffle back step, using one of three methods: move the rear foot first with front foot following, move the front foot back first with rear foot following, or slide both feet backward at the same time.

Drill 2   Execute a pulling back step.

Drill 3   Take one step backward but don't change your position. Keep your weight on your rear foot and be ready for the kick after you step back.

Drill 4   Turn 180 degrees to the rear (front foot circles to the rear with torso facing forward as opposed to turning backward) and face your opponent. Return to your original position (reverse tornado).

This drill can be applied to a multitude of stepping techniques. In a group setting, students line up facing one direction. They bounce in place with feinting motions. As a whole, the class shuffles back two times. Everyone turns, changes direction, and shuffles back to complete one set. After completing one set, switch to another step (for example, switch from the shuffle back step to the pulling back step). Continue with additional steps until you have executed 10 sets.

Step Round Knee Kicks (Counter)

This is a beginning technique that is good for correcting body position for kicks and assists in balance, coordination, and speed. Because you do not execute the full kick, your speed increases and you can focus on correcting your stance and torso position.

Drill 1   Execute a shuffle back step with a rear-knee round kick. Drop your foot forward and shuffle back. Switch feet and execute another knee kick. Drop your foot forward and shuffle back.

Drill 2   Execute a pulling back step with a front- or rear-knee round kick. After executing the pulling back step, raise the front knee as if to kick. Drop it forward and then execute a pulling back step. Raise the leg for a rear-knee kick, drop it forward, and switch directions, completing one set.

Drill 3   Take one step back and execute a rear-knee round kick. Step straight back one step (left foot), keeping body position forward and weight on the right foot. Execute a rear-knee kick (left leg), drop it forward, and repeat. After repeating 10 times in one direction, turn and switch directions.

Drill 4   Turn 180 degrees clockwise with a rear-knee round kick. Drop it forward and return to the original position.

Shift your weight back and forth after any back step so that you are ready for the knee kick. This drill can be applied to a multitude of stepping techniques. Additional kicks could be incorporated into the drill such as axe kicks, pushing kicks, jump spin back kicks, spin hook kicks, and tornado kicks (turn 180 degrees).

In a group setting, students line up facing one direction. As a group, the class practices the drills together. After completing one set of a particular step, switch to another step (for example, go from a shuffle back step to a pulling back step). Perform 10 sets, continuing through all of the steps.

Steps With Partner (Counter)

This drill focuses on target accuracy, distance control, reaction timing, balance, weight shifts, and footwork for countermovements.

The following examples provide an idea of how this drill might be practiced. A variety of combinations is possible.

Drill 1   Both partners execute a switch-foot step.

Drill 2   Partner A performs a forward shuffle step while partner B performs a shuffle back step.

Drill 3   Partner A performs a pulling in step while partner B performs a pulling back step.

Drill 4   Partner A performs one step in while partner B performs one step back.

Drill 5   Partner A performs a running step in while partner B performs a pulling back step.

Drill 6   Both partners turn 180 degrees clockwise and 180 degrees back to their original position.

Partners face each other and execute drills back and forth. In a group setting, two lines of students face each other. Bounce in place with feinting motions. For each drill, partner A executes a forward stepping motion while partner B executes a reverse stepping motion.

Practice each drill in sets of 10 repetitions. The back-and-forth executions give each student practice in attack and counterattack steps. Continue through all of the steps.

Counterkicks With Partner

Counterkick with partner drills (figure 9.3) work on reaction time, distance control, quick footwork, agility, and target accuracy.

The following examples are just a few ideas of how this drill might be practiced. A variety of combinations can be used. These drills can incorporate

Figure 9.3 A variety of kicks can be incorporated into counterkick with partner drills.

many step and counterstep sets such as axe kicks, pushing kicks, jump spin back kicks, spin hook kicks, and tornado kicks (180-degree turn).

Drill 1 Partner A attacks with a rear round kick with or without a shuffle step in. Partner B counterattacks with a rear round kick with a shuffle step back.

Drill 2 Partner A attacks with a switch-foot step, a fast pulling step, one step forward, or a running step with a rear round kick. Partner B counterattacks by taking one step back with the front (left) foot and counterkicking with that foot or opting for a jump spin hook kick or jump spin back kick using the right foot.

Drill 3 Partner A attacks with a fast front round kick (pulling step). Partner B counterattacks by turning 180 degrees to the rear with one step to the back, then facing forward and launching a rear round kick (reverse tornado).

For each drill, partners face each other in sparring stance. In a group setting, two lines of students face each other. Begin with bouncing in place or steps with feinting motions of the entire body, hands, and feet. Partner A executes a forward-step motion, and partner B executes a reverse-step motion. Forward motion constitutes two motions—the step forward and the kick. The counterattack constitutes one or two motions. The combined motions of partner A and partner B make up one set. Partner B's counterreaction is triggered when partner A drops the kick forward. At that moment, partner B launches the counterkick. Reaction timing is an important aspect of this drill.

Practice each drill in sets of 10 repetitions. The back-and-forth executions provide practice in attack and counterattack steps. Continue with additional drills as noted.

Paddle Kicks With Partner (Counter)

For this drill, you will need paddles, either one or two per target holder, and a body shield. This drill develops reaction time, distance control, power, follow-through, and target accuracy. The chest protection comes into play during the spin back kicks. The other kicks can be done using the paddles.

Drill 1   Execute a shuffle back step and a rear round kick. Drop your foot forward and return to your original position after the kick.

Drill 2   Take one step back and execute a rear round kick.

Drill 3   Execute a front-foot axe kick in place by executing a pulling half-step backward with the front foot and then executing the axe kick.

Drill 4   Turn 180 degrees clockwise and execute a rear round kick.

Drill 5   Execute a spin back kick in place or shuffle back step with a short jump spin back kick.

Drill 6   Execute a spin hook kick in place with a shuffle back step.

This drill requires two people, one of whom has either one or two target paddles and a ho gu, or body shield, for protection from back kicks. The kicker stands in ready position. The paddle holder simulates an attack by thrusting forward a paddle in a high or low position. The kicker must react to the target.

The emphasis is target accuracy. The kicker needs to concentrate on reacting to the paddle as it comes forward and focusing power through the target. Each time a kick is launched, the kicker drops the kick forward and then returns to the original position by either shuffling back or cross-stepping backward.

The kicker executes a set of specific drills and then switches with the target holder.

Chest Pad With Partner (Counter)

For this drill, both partners need to wear a chest pad. This drill focuses on target accuracy, contact power, sense of contact, follow-through, distance control, gross motor coordination, balance, weight shifts, and footwork.

Drill 1   Partner A attacks with a rear round kick with or without a shuffle step in. Partner B counterattacks with a rear round kick with a shuffle step back.

Drill 2   Partner A attacks with a switch-foot step; a fast (pulling) step; one step forward; or a running step with a rear round kick, axe kick, or pushing kick. Partner B counterattacks by taking one step back with the front (left) foot and executing a round kick (left).

Drill 3   Partner A attacks with a fast front round kick (pulling step). Partner B counterattacks with a jump spin back kick or spin hook kick or else turns

180 degrees to the rear and takes one step to the back and then faces forward and launches a rear round kick.

These drills can incorporate many step and counterstep sets such as axe kicks, pushing kicks, jump spin back kicks, or spin hook kicks.

Partners face each other in sparring stance. In a group setting, two lines of students face each other. Begin by bouncing in place or feinting. When partner A executes a kick, partner B executes a counterkick. The kick and counterkick constitute one set. Practice each drill in sets of 10 repetitions. The back-and-forth executions give each student practice in attacking and counterattacking. Continue with additional drills as noted.

Partner B's counterattack is triggered when partner A drops the kick forward. At that moment, partner B launches the counterkick. Reaction time is an important aspect of this drill.

This is a full-contact drill. Focus on feeling the effects of the kick as it is executed. Read your opponent's reaction and timing. Do not use blocks; this is just practice.

Kicking Bag (Counter)

For this drill, you will need a floor kicking bag or hanging bag. Instead of a bag, you can have a partner hold a body shield as a target or wear a chest pad supplemented with two paddles for protection. Power and target accuracy are the main lessons for this drill.

Drill 1   Execute a shuffle back step and a round kick.

Drill 2   Punch with or without additional steps or kicks.

Drill 3   Execute a jump spin back kick either in place or with a shuffle back step.

Drill 4   Execute tornado kicks.

Drill 5   Execute jump spin hook kicks at a paddle or the bag.

Line up behind the bag or target. Take turns executing specific counterattacking motions and return to end of the line. Any of the previously covered counteractions can be used. This is an opportunity to exercise power in the kick or punch without risking injury to your partner.

SIDE-STEP DRILLS (COUNTER)

Side steps are useful when sparring with an opponent who has an attacking style. You want to be able to sidestep an attack, break the forward rhythm of your opponent, and counter from different angles other than straight back. Side steps are excellent for counterattacks. The sense of body position is different from a backward retreat and often requires hip rotation and pivoting. These drills should help with that process.

Basic Side Steps

Your weight shift is important when moving to the side. Generally, balance and weight are shifted in the direction of the sideways step and then quickly shifted in the direction of the attack.

In a group setting, students line up facing one direction. As a group, the class moves twice to the right and twice to the left. This constitutes one set. After completing one set, switch to another step (for example, the pulling step with kick). Continue with additional steps until you have executed 10 sets.

Drill 1   Step side to side, two steps in a row. The left foot steps first, and the right foot follows. Repeat for two steps. Next, the right foot moves first and then the left foot follows. Keep steps about shoulder-width apart.

Drill 2   Step side to side with pulling steps and a knee kick or round kick. Step left to right and right to left, each time aiming your kick to the center. You will need to rotate the hip for the kick.

Drill 3   Execute a twist back step (basic counterstep). The front foot replaces the rear foot. The rear foot rises for a knee or round kick. The upper body leans back and the hip and torso twist in the direction of the kick.

Advanced Side Steps and Knee Round Kicks

The drills for advanced side steps include movements that involve pivoting the feet and rotating the torso. These drills build upon the basic side-step drills for weight shifts, balance, and quickness, and they add a dimension of twisting and hip rotation for changing directions.

In a group setting, students line up facing one direction. As a whole, the class executes the step in one direction and then reverses direction. This constitutes one set. After completing one set of a particular step, switch to another step. Continue with additional steps until you have executed 10 sets.

Drill 1   Step with your rear foot 45 or 90 degrees to the side. Pivot clockwise on your front foot.

Drill 2   Step with your rear foot 45 or 90 degrees to the side. Pivot counterclockwise on your front foot.

Drill 3   Your rear foot moves forward and to the side while the front foot (left) is simultaneously pulling to the right. Rotate the hip and execute a right-knee round kick.

Drill 4   Take one step at a 45-degree angle back to the left with the front (left) foot. The rear (right) foot pulls toward the left foot at the same time. Rotate the hip for a left-knee (round) kick.

Side-Step Knee Round Kicks With Partner

The following drills work on timing, weight shifts, balance, and reaction.

Partners face each other in sparring stance. In a group setting, two lines of students face each other. Begin with bouncing in place or feinting. When partner A executes a kick, partner B executes a counterkick. The kick and counterkick constitute one set. Practice each drill in sets of 10 repetitions. The back-and-forth executions give each student practice in attacking and counter-attacking. Remember to switch feet and practice the drill with the other foot forward. Continue with additional drills as noted. In this instance, partners are not wearing protection; therefore, there is no contact. Distance and accuracy are still important and kicks should be directed correctly at the target. Although no contact is made, each partner should practice the appropriate arm block when the counterkick is executed.

Drill 1   Partner A attacks with a rear round kick, rear axe kick, or rear spin back kick. Partner B counters with a front-foot twist 45 degrees toward the rear foot and a rear round kick. Or, partner B can counter by stepping the rear foot 45 or 90 degrees to the side and pivoting counterclockwise on the front foot.

Drill 2   Partner A attacks with a pulling step and a front round kick or pushing kick or with a running step in with a round kick. Partner B counters by stepping the rear foot 45 or 90 degrees to the side and pivoting clockwise on the front foot. Or, partner B can counter by taking one step 45 degrees to the back with the front foot and executing a rear round kick or a jump spin back kick right after the back step.

Drill 3   Partner A attacks with a fast front round kick. Partner B counters by turning clockwise 180 degrees to the back and executing a jump spin rear-knee round kick.

Paddle Kicks With Partner

Paddle kicks help improve timing, weight shifts, balance, power control, angle of reaction to the attack, and target accuracy.

Drill 1   Step side to side and execute a round kick (front foot to side and kick with same foot).

Drill 2   Take a twist back step (basic counterstep). The front foot pulls to the rear foot as the hips rotate for a switch round kick. The upper body leans back.

Drill 3   Step with the rear foot 45 or 90 degrees to the left side, passing behind the front foot. Pivot clockwise on the front foot. Perform a rear round kick with the right foot.

Drill 4   Step with the rear foot 45 or 90 degrees to the right side. Pivot counterclockwise on the front foot. Perform a rear round kick with the right foot (figure 9.4).

Figure 9.4   Partner provides a target with a paddle for a rear round kick with the right foot.

Drill 5   Step with the rear foot 45 degrees forward and to the side. Slide the front (left) foot to the side and execute a round kick with the right foot.

Drill 6   With the front (left) foot, take one step back at a 45-degree angle to the left. Pull the rear (right) foot toward the left foot at the same time and hop to switch support. Rotate the hip and execute a left-knee (round) kick with a twist step.

Drill 7   Pivot on the rear foot, turning 180 degrees clockwise to the back. With the front foot, step to the rear and continue to rotate forward. Slide the front (right) foot back toward the left foot. Kick with the left foot (bada chagi).

Drill 8   Execute a spin hook kick or a jump spin hook kick in place.

Face your partner. Your partner should hold one or two paddles. The holder determines the direction and presentation of the paddle. A quick, surprise presentation helps to develop reaction time and target accuracy. The focus is on the 45- or 90-degree side-step counterattack. The holder should angle the paddle so that the kicker has to use side-step techniques.

Chest-Pad Kicks

The following drills help to hone timing, weight shifts, balance, power control, reaction angle to the attack, and target accuracy. Contact in practice should be as realistic as possible.

Partners face each other in sparring stance. In a group setting, two lines of students face each other. Begin with bouncing in place or feinting. When partner A executes a kick, partner B executes a counterkick. The kick and counterkick constitute one set. Practice each drill in sets of 10 repetitions. The back-and-forth executions give each student practice in attacking and counterattacking. Continue with additional drills as noted.

Partner B's best counterreaction is triggered when partner A's kick is at its zenith in the air and beginning to drop. At that moment, partner B launches the counterkick. Reaction time is an important aspect of this drill.

This is a full-contact drill. Focus on feeling the kick as it is executed and feeling the effects of the attack. Read your opponent's reaction and timing. Do not use arm blocks.

Drill 1   Partner A attacks with a rear round kick, rear axe kick, or rear spin back kick. Partner B counters with a 45-degree front-foot twist step to the right toward the rear foot and a simultaneous rear round kick. Or, partner B can counter with a 45- or 90-degree step to the side with the rear foot and a pivot counterclockwise on the front foot and follow with a round or double round kick. The attack is coming on the left side, so you want to step to the right out of the way and attack your partner's open side.

Drill 2   Partner A attacks with a pulling step and a front round kick or pushing kick or else with a running step and a rear round kick. Partner B counters by stepping the rear foot 45 or 90 degrees to the side and pivoting clockwise on the front foot. Or, partner B can counter by taking the front foot one step back at a 45-degree angle and executing a rear round kick or jump spin back kick. The attack is coming on the right side, so you want to step left out of the way and attack your partner's open side.

Drill 3   Partner A attacks with a fast front round kick. Partner B counters by pivoting on the rear foot and turning clockwise 180 degrees to the back (reverse tornado). With the front foot, partner B steps to the rear, circling clockwise. Partner B's back will be to partner A only for a moment. Quickly partner B rotates forward and then slides the front (right) foot back toward the left foot and kicks with the left foot (bada chagi) after partner A lands the round kick.

Kicking Bag

Every drill discussed to this point could be adapted to the kicking bag with a focus on delivery of power. The following examples are just a few of the many possibilities. The focus is exercising full power for kicks and punches.

Line up behind the bag or target. Take turns executing specific counterattacking motions and return to the end of the line. Any of the previously covered counteractions can be used. This is an opportunity to exercise power in the kick or punch without risking injury to your partner. If there are enough bags for everyone, practice one on one with a bag.

Drill 1   Step to the right, and with your left hand, execute a low block and then a right punch. Reverse directions and step to the left, use your right hand for a low block, and perform a left punch.

Drill 2   Circle the bag and execute a rear round kick counterclockwise and a front round kick clockwise.

Drill 3   Take a twist back step and execute a rear round kick at the same time (bada chagi). The front foot pulls to the rear and the hip rotates for the kick. The upper body leans back.

Drill 4   Moving counterclockwise, step at a 45-degree angle to the side with the rear foot and then slide the front foot to where the rear foot was. Execute a rear round kick right after stepping to the side.

Drill 5   With the front foot, take one step back at a 45-degree angle. Execute a rear round kick right after stepping back. The rear foot pulls to the left and the hip rotates for a left-foot round kick.

Drill 6   Perform a reverse tornado. Pivot on your rear foot, turning clockwise 180 degrees to the back. Continue rotating forward. Slide your front (right) foot back toward your left foot. Kick with your left foot (counterkick).

Drill 7   Step with the rear foot 45 or 90 degrees clockwise. Pivot on the front foot and kick with the front foot.

BASIC KICK COMBINATIONS

Basic kick combinations consist of two or three motions. You will need a partner to practice these combinations in drills. Focus on shifting your weight quickly and improving your balance, flexibility, and automatic actions.

Basic Kick Combinations With Partner

Set up the drills as line drills, or simply face your partner (figure 9.5). For line drills, each line takes turns executing combinations back and forth. Focus on speed and target accuracy.

Drill 1   Perform all basic kicks as knee kicks with fast steps, running steps, or one step forward. You can execute the full kick.

Drill 2   With a partner, perform combination knee kicks with two or three knee-kick motions, such as the following:

- Round kick, round kick; or, round kick, double round kick (rear foot first)
- Round kick, spin back kick

Figure 9.5 Face your partner for basic kick combinations.

- Pushing kick, round kick
- Rear round kick (more of a fake), double round kick
- Basic forward attack step with knee round kick or round kick
- Switch-foot step with rear-knee round kick or round kick
- Shuffle step in with rear-knee round kick or round kick
- Pulling step with front-knee round kick or round kick
- One step forward with rear-knee round kick or round kick
- Hop-jump step with rear-knee axe kick or axe kick
- Running step with rear-knee round kick or round kick
- 180-degree clockwise turn with rear-knee round kick or round kick
- Rear-foot cut kick with skipping combined with any kick

Drill 3   Perform a combination knee kick and step with a partner. Some combination options are the pulling step with round kick, running step with round or axe kick, pulling round kick with spin back, foot switch and knee kick, and one step forward (or knee slightly up) and spin back kick.

Basic Kick Combinations With Paddles

For these drills, you will need two paddles and a partner. Focus on distance control, target accuracy, follow-through, balance, flexibility, reaction, timing, and power control. Any steps and basic kicks can be combined into two or three techniques.

Face your partner in a sparring stance. Your partner uses two paddles to lead the target for you. Kick the target and rechamber to your original position quickly. Repeat and take turns. These drills can also be performed as line drills. Start the line at the end of the gym and take turns returning.

Drill 1   Before your double round kick, with or without a jump, execute one of these options:

- In place, take your rear foot to your partner's trunk or face.
- Switch your feet and take your rear foot to your partner's trunk or face.
- Take one step forward or a running step and take your rear foot to your partner's trunk or face.

Drill 2   Before your front double or triple round kick, execute a pulling step, with or without a jump, or fake with your front foot and take your rear foot to your partner's trunk or face.

Drill 3   Perform a cut kick with double round kicks.

Drill 4   Execute a tornado kick with double round kicks.

Basic Kick Combinations With Partner (Counter)

For these drills, you will need a chest pad and a partner. Practice your fake motions with whole-body actions to experience the reaction from your partner. Focus on quickly shifting your weight and improving your timing, accuracy, and distance control.

These drills can be done as line drills (two lines face each other). Start lines at one end of the gym. Span the length of the gym and return. If you are working with a partner, face your partner in sparring stance. When your partner attacks, you counterattack. The attack and counterattack constitute one set. Counterattacks should be triggered when the attacker drops the kick forward. At that moment, launch the counterkick. Reaction timing is an important aspect of these drills.

Practice each drill in sets of 10. The back-and-forth executions give each student practice in attack and counterattack steps. Although only a few drills are included, there are many changeable situations in the competition arena. Experience plays an important part in setting a practice goal.

Although round kicks are used in the following drills, other kicks—axe kicks, back kicks, spin hook kicks, and pushing kicks—could be used in the attacks and counterattacks. Blocks and fist techniques can also be integrated into the drills.

Drill 1   Partner A attacks with a rear round kick and another round kick. Partner B's counterattack is a rear punch with a clinch and a rear round kick or jump spin back kick.

Drill 2   This drill features a combination attack. Partner A attacks with a rear round kick and rear round or double round kick and then takes the rear foot to partner B's trunk or face. For the counterattack, partner B executes a jump back or spin hook kick either in place or with a shuffle back step (one or two steps).

Drill 3 The combination attack features a fast double round kick with a pulling step to the front. The attacker takes the rear foot to the partner's trunk or face. For the counterattack, perform a shuffle step back with a twist step. The front foot pulls to the rear foot with a twist to the back. At the same time, execute a rear round kick.

LINE DRILLS:
FORWARD MOTION (RUNNING) KICKS

The following drills will help correct kick and step techniques and build speed, momentum, and balance. You will improve speed and agility; develop a sense of your center of gravity; and increase flexibility, coordination, and endurance.

The most common drills are described, although the combinations are endless. The basic premise for practice is running the length of the dojang while executing the kick. This allows for forward motion while incorporating a technique. Greater concentration is required as additional steps and kicks are combined.

Running Knee and Basic Kicks

Knee kicks are an elementary way to combine advanced motions. Here we will focus on just raising the knee to the correct position without executing the kick. Concentrate on correct body and foot position.

The class lines up in kicking lines. Each student assumes the sparring stance at an imaginary starting line with a set distance to cover within the room, gym, or dojang. If there is more than one line of students, all students start behind the imaginary starting line. Students execute basic knee kicks from the starting line to the finish line and full leg kicks as they return to the starting line. Or, after finishing the basic knee kicks, students return to the starting line and do backward counterkicks instead.

After performing the drill in one direction and reaching the opposite wall, students prepare to return. They rechamber to sparring stance to begin the next drill and repeat the drill as they return to the starting line.

Remember to keep your knees flexible so your body weight can shift forward quickly with momentum. Spring up using the knee and bottom of the foot. Also, twist at the waist and rotate the hip to help launch the kick.

Keep the upper body flexible and loose. Allow the arms to swing and contribute to the forward momentum to help increase speed. Relaxation of the body will increase flexibility, height, distance, and balance. The body should recoil like a spring during these exercises.

Drill 1   This drill uses one motion for basic kicks. Perform basic knee kicks or round kicks such as knee front kicks, knee round kicks, or knee back kicks.

Drill 2   This drill uses two or three motions, combining kicks with feinting motions. Perform a full-body fake motion with multiple combination kicks, such as the following:

- Round kick, round kick
- Round kick, double round kick (rear foot first)
- Round kick, spin back kick
- Cut or pushing kick, round kick

Drill 3   This drill uses two or three motions, combining kicks with feinting motions and steps. Perform basic kicks as the knee kick or full kick and include steps or fakes, such as the following:

- Rear round kick (more of a fake), double round kick
- Bounding (1, 2, 3) with round kick
- Switch-foot step with rear-knee round kick or round kick
- Forward shuffle step with rear-knee round kick or round kick
- Fast or pulling step with front-knee round kick or round kick
- One step forward with rear-knee round kick or round kick
- Hop-jump step with rear-knee axe kick or axe kick
- Running step with rear-knee round kick or round kick
- 180-degree clockwise turn with rear-knee round kick or round kick (tornado kick)
- Rear-foot cut or pushing kick with skipping combined with any kick

Drill 4   This drill uses two or more motions, combining fakes and steps. Shuffle forward steps can be used in combination as in these examples:

- Shuffle forward step with rear round kick or double round kicks (rear foot to trunk or face)
- Shuffle forward step with punching and jump spin back kick or jump spin hook kick (right hand and rear foot to trunk or face)

Switch-foot steps can be used in combination as in these examples:

- Switch-foot step with double knee round kicks (rear foot to trunk or face)
- Switch-foot step, cut or pushing kick with rear foot with double knee round kick (rear foot to trunk or face)

- Switch-foot step, cut kick with rear foot with jump spin back kick or jump spin hook kick (rear foot to trunk or face)

Pulling or fast steps can be used in combination as in these examples:

- Pulling step with double or triple front-knee round kicks (rear foot to trunk or face)
- Pulling step with double front-knee round kicks (front or rear foot to trunk or face) with spin
- Pulling step with fast front-knee round kick with spin back kick (front or rear foot to trunk or face)

One step forward can be used in combination with the running step. Add a double knee round kick with the rear foot to the trunk or face or a double round kick with a jump spin back kick.

Finally, turn 180 degrees clockwise with a double knee round kick (rear foot to the trunk or face). Combine with the axe kick, back kick, spin hook kick, cut kick, or pushing kick.

Running Sparring

Training with running sparring will improve competition skill and your ability to make snap judgments in the ring.

Use all of the skill sets that have been covered to this point. Any variety of combinations can be used. For example, two students could take turns as the attacker, incorporating all kicks, steps, and punches. Set up a line drill as follows:

- One attack and one countermove, such as attack by rear round, counter with rear round kick with twist step
- Two attacks and one countermove, such as attack by double round kick, counter with jump spin back or jump spin hook kick
- One attack and two countermoves, such as attack by rear round kick, counter by right punch and jump spin back kick
- One attack, one countermove, and one re-countermove, such as attack by rear round, counter by rear round kick, rechamber and reattack by jump spin back or spin hook kick

For the line drill, fighters face each other in lines and do sparring drills. The first line moves backward, blocking and countering, as the second line attacks. All this is done as the fighters in the second line move forward toward the end of the space. Once they reach the end of the space, fighters reverse positions and go back to the starting point. Use knee kicks rather than full kicks for this drill. The focus is reaction time and automatic response to certain attack or counterattack situations.

STEP SPARRING AND KNEE SPARRING

Step sparring and knee sparring simulate competition circumstances and improve reaction time, attacking timing, agility, endurance, and distance control. Expect to improve your speed as you shift your weight back and forth. Practice scoring techniques.

With a partner, perform step sparring, one on one, with no contact. Simulate sparring using knee and footwork actions instead of full kicks. Practice blocking and distance control. Because there is no contact, no pads are necessary.

KICKING-BAG SPARRING

In kicking-bag sparring, you respond to imaginary attacks to improve target accuracy and power development as well as delivery of kicks and punches.

You will need a kicking bag. In timed segments, attack and counterattack the bag using speed and power. All manner of kicks and punches can be used; the point is to mix it up and work continuously for a set amount of time, such as one or two minutes. Moves might include the following:

- Rear round kick, bring it back, and jump spin back or hook kick
- Move to side, round kick or double round
- Clinch bag, step back, and double round kick
- Clinch bag, punch, and jump spin back kick

INTENSIFIED TRAINING DRILLS

Intensified training drills take you to the next level of endurance. With basic movements in place, we build on intensity by focusing on speed of performance, learning to quickly change directions, and enduring nonstop blocks without rest, all of which help increase stamina for competition. You want to be ready to participate in more than one match without losing your energy. If you are a winner, several matches at an event may be a reality.

One-on-One Paddle Target Training

Paddle target training will increase your ability to quickly shift your center of gravity. You will also improve muscle endurance, agility, explosive power, and capacity to endure exertion. For one-on-one training, you need a partner and a paddle.

The holder stands to the side with a paddle. The kicker kicks through the target, turns around, and performs the next drill, attacking through the target each time using the following techniques in a circuit:

Drill 1   Perform a cut kick with both the front foot and rear foot with punching.

Drill 2   Perform an axe kick with both the front foot and rear foot.

Drill 3   Perform a pushing kick while staying in place, taking one step forward, or taking running steps.

Drill 4   Perform a pushing kick with both the front foot and rear foot.

Drill 5   Perform an axe kick while staying in place, taking a pulling step, taking one step forward, or taking running steps.

Drill 6   Perform a back kick with the rear foot either while staying in place, taking a pulling step, taking one step forward, or taking running steps.

Decide what the set will consist of before beginning the drills. The set may be one skill or many. Each person does the entire set before moving on to the next set. Perform each set for a preset time such as 30 or 60 seconds. After finishing the entire circuit, change holders.

Two-on-One Paddle Target Training

Like one-on-one paddle target training, two-on-one paddle target training will increase your speed as you shift your center of gravity. It will also improve muscle endurance, agility, and explosive power. You will need two partners, each with one paddle (figure 9.6).

Figure 9.6   For two-on-one paddle drills, you will need two partners, each with a paddle to use as a target.

Drill 1 Begin with round kicks:

- Round kick with rear foot while standing in place or after switching feet
- Round kick with rear foot after a shuffle step
- Round kick with front foot after a pulling step or running step
- Cut kick with the front or rear foot and rear round kick

Drill 2 Perform axe kicks:

- Axe kick with front or rear foot while standing in place or after a pulling step
- Axe kick with the rear foot after a running step or a hop-jump step
- Cut kick with the front or rear foot with a crescent axe kick

Drill 3 Perform back kicks:

- Back kick with rear foot while standing in place or after switching feet
- Back kick with rear foot after taking one step forward
- Cut kick with front or rear foot with a back kick

Drill 4 Perform a spin hook kick while standing in place, after switching feet, or after taking a shuffle step back.

Drill 5 Perform double round kicks:

- Double round kick to the trunk or face with the rear foot while standing in place
- Double round kick to the trunk or face with the rear foot after switching feet
- Double round kick to the trunk or face with the rear foot after a shuffle step
- Double round kick to the trunk or face with the front or rear foot after a pulling step
- Double round kick to the trunk or face with the rear foot after a running step
- Cut kick with the front or rear foot and double round kick to the trunk or face with the rear foot

There are two holders with the kicker in the middle. Use the listed techniques in a circuit fashion. After each person finishes the circuit, switch holders. Use a set time of 30 or 60 seconds to finish the circuit before switching roles.

Paddle Sparring

One person holds two paddles and quickly initiates various target positions for the attacker to respond to with kicks or punches (figure 9.7). Paddle spar-

Figure 9.7 Partner creates targets with two paddles.

ring will improve the speed at which you shift your weight. It will also train muscle endurance, agility, concentration, timing, reaction time, and hand and foot coordination.

The holder has two paddles and determines the skill to be trained by changing the angle of the paddle target, the speed of presentation, and the direction of presentation to simulate feints and steps for all basic and advanced kicks. Set a time limit of 60 seconds for two or three rounds with 30-second breaks. The holder leads the presentation and should concentrate on simulating movement in the ring so the kicker can be exposed to various angles of attack and counterattack.

Chest-Pad Kicks

For chest-pad kicks, participants should wear a chest pad or hold a body shield.

Drill 1: Impact Noise Drill   The impact noise drill will develop kicking accuracy so that the kick to the ho gu will create a louder sound. Both fighters should wear chest pads. The holder should place two paddles under the chest pad for additional protection. The holder is in sparring position except she will not use her hands to block; her hands should secure the placement of the paddles. The kicker strikes the chest pad with a round kick, adjusting as necessary to create the most noise. There is no defense against the kicks. This drill can be done one on one (both wearing pads), two on one with one person kicking and the two holders wearing pads, or with several students taking turns attacking one target person who counters their attacks.

Drill 2: Counterattack Drill   The counterattack drill will help you develop automatic responses to attacks. You will learn to read your opponent's reactions, developing timing, distance control, target accuracy, and power. This is a good drill to develop automatic responses to certain situations and to develop your expertise. Two options might be used. In both options, everyone wears pads.

In option 1, the kicker responds to several attacks. Students line up and present different attacks—rear-leg round kicks, various rear attacks, front fast kicks, spin attacks—to the counterattacker. After the attack and counterattack, the attacker moves to the end of the line and the next student presents a different attack. When the line is finished, the counterattacker joins the attack line and another student takes the counterattack position.

Option 2 uses two lines of students. The students face each other. The students in line 1 deliver random attacks or a specific set of attacks, and the students in line 2 counter each move. The focus might be on rear-leg attacks, spin back attacks, or front-foot attacks with the various counters that work in those situations. Rotation can occur after a predetermined amount of time or after a specific set of attacks and counters have been performed.

Free Sparring

Free sparring is designed to simulate competition, including rule and time limitations. Focus on balance, weight shifts, and feints. Free sparring will build agility, endurance, reaction time, reflexes, and speed, and it will improve physical conditioning. Fighters should wear chest pads to minimize contact. Fighters are in closed stance, looking at each other. Fighters can use single or combination attacks and basic or advanced steps and kicks.

In the first option (one on one), one student is the initiator and creates various sparring situations so the other student can counterattack. The initiator does not kick but only presents body positions and footwork for the other student to react to.

The second method is three on one or four on one. Three or four students go against one student. Everyone is in sparring position and attacks the defender with different techniques. Any technique is OK. This helps to develop speed and reaction time.

The third option is also one-on-one sparring, but in a class setting. Everyone should be geared up and sitting in a big circle. Two people are in the center performing free sparring. The person who scores first gets to sit down. The other fighter has to stay up and fight the next person in line.

The fourth option can be one on one or two on one. It is simulation sparring with timed rounds (one minute, two rounds; two minutes, three rounds).

SKILL TRAINING AND CONDITIONING

Now you have finished the basic drills. Your foundation of knowledge and skill should be solid. So where do you go from here? These next few sections help you "ice the cake." You won't find these methods anywhere else. From my years of experience in the national and international arena, I have found that these exercises help take athletes over the top. This level is where you smooth the rough edges of your training and hone your style, making your movements more natural. Here is the push for intensity, speed, and that extra something that is yours alone.

Raising the Knee

This exercise will develop strength in the quadriceps and flexibility in the hamstrings. It also will increase the speed of your fast kick.

Run in place, raising your knees high. Place your hands level over your knees and begin slowly, touching your knees to your hands. Go slowly for 5 to 10 seconds and then increase to a fast running speed for 5 to 10 seconds. Keep this up for at least 60 seconds. As you become better conditioned, increase your time in 30-second increments.

Twisting the Waist and Hip

Developing flexibility and power in the waist will help you generate speed and power for kicks and develop your distance techniques.

From a fighting stance at a slight angle, move the hips straight forward and slightly twist in the direction of a kick delivery. The rear knee should be facing forward. Follow through with the kick.

If you need to close a gap, while rotating the hips forward move the body forward for more power. The upper body leans back slightly. You may have to lean out of the way of an attack while delivering your own, which takes extreme balance and a long reach. Remember to twist the waist during this motion. If you don't get the rotation on the hip, your kick has less power and your upright torso becomes a nice target for your opponent. Don't just raise the knee and snap the leg. Pivot on the ball of the supporting foot. As the hip moves forward, the upper body will lean back slightly. Use the motion of the hip and the twist of the body to provide power to the kick.

Feinting

The purpose of feinting is to secure the upper hand in the match and confuse your opponent by hiding your main strategy, thus creating a chance to attack. Use all hand, foot, and body feinting motions; attacking kick feints with punching; cut-kick stepping feints; spinning feints; and back kick feints to draw in your opponent.

Train for feints by standing in front of a mirror so that you can see if you look like you are actually committing to the attack. While bounding, execute fake lunges, kicks, or moves to confuse the opponent. Put energy into your movements. Move quickly and blend actions. Build your own drills or practice random, spontaneous movements in front of the mirror. You need to know how your movements look to the opponent. Are you convincing? Are you fast enough to elicit a reaction and to quickly make your move? Here are some examples.

Drill 1   Bound on the balls of the feet, then feint a punch forward with a stepping check motion. Shift backward.

Drill 2   Move the whole body in a forward checking motion with hands and feet, then quickly shift backward a step.

Drill 3   Slide the front foot forward in a checking motion, then slide or step back to your original position.

Drill 4   Launch a front-foot low fake kick and take a front-foot side step at the same time. Kick to the opponent with the same foot or launch a rear-leg low fake kick, take a side step, and set the foot down momentarily before launching a kick with the same foot.

Stepping

It is necessary to develop good balance and the ability to shift your center of weight as quickly as possible while moving your feet.

Relax the entire body, especially the shoulders. Begin bouncing on the balls of your feet. Make sudden shifts in foot position. For example, if you are in a left fighting stance bouncing on the balls of your feet, change to a right fighting stance. Slide your feet and do not lift them off the floor. Move as quickly as possible. Use this same exercise with all types of stepping motions such as side, forward, back, and pyramid steps.

The more advanced version of this exercise uses combinations of steps in random order. Regardless of the steps you use, be sure to do the exercise with as much speed as possible.

Drill 1   Slide two feet backward at the same time or step backward with the left foot, pivoting on the rear foot, or combine the two.

Drill 2   Pivot on the front foot as the rear foot moves to the side at a 45- or 90-degree angle.

Drill 3   Take multiple steps, combining at least two steps in a drill—forward, backward, side to side, and so on.

Kicking

Review the basic kicks. Correct the kick positions. Check foot pivot, balance, and weight shift.

Perform a front snap kick. Raise the left knee high, keeping the foot tucked under the body. Turn the knee and bring the foot forward in a snapping motion. Snap the foot back to its starting position as quickly as possibly with the knee still raised. Hold the knee up and do the exercise again.

Repeat this exercise with every basic kick. Review body position, delivery of kick, knee position, and foot stance and balance.

Cut Kicking and Balance

These exercises will help you develop proper weight shifts and delivery location of the kick.

Drill 1   Raise the knee high. Quickly snap the kick out and back. Keep the knee raised and pivot on the supporting foot 90 degrees clockwise. Again, snap the kick out and then in as quickly as possible. Repeat this process to complete the circle such that you are turning your torso on the supporting leg without setting down the kicking leg. Also perform the exercise in a counterclockwise direction. Do this exercise in 30-second increments and then switch feet.

Drill 2   From a fighting stance, bring the rear foot forward into a cut kick. Shift your upper-body weight forward for kick delivery. Maintain balance. Rechamber your leg and repeat.

Drill 3   From a fighting stance, raise the front foot for a cut kick. Shift your upper-body weight back to the rear leg.

Adding Distance

These exercises will help you add distance to cut kicks, pushing kicks, and axe kicks. Learn to add a skip or hop in order to cover distance to your opponent and improve balance.

To cover distance, raise the front knee high. At the same time, skip forward on the supporting foot so that your kick will land on the target that is away from you. By throwing the knee up, you give yourself forward momentum. On a high kick, the knee should come all the way up to the chest. Balance will also be preserved by doing the skip at the same time as the knee is raised.

For rear-leg delivery, bring the rear leg forward and raise the leg to the position of the kick being delivered. At the same time, skip or hop forward on the supporting leg to close the gap.

Training for Speed

These exercises will develop speed and timing for competition, increase agility, and build heart and lung endurance.

The first exercise trains blocking, snap kicks, round kicks, and high kicks. Stand facing your partner. Both of you kick with the left foot and rechamber the foot, setting it down next to the supporting foot. Step back with the supporting foot and launch the kick with it. This will cause you to switch feet with every kick. Your partner does the same movement. Each of you blocks the other person's kick. You should both move at the same speed and at the same time. In the same fashion, practice any combination of kicks, steps, and blocks. Work toward improving timing, speed, distance, and accuracy.

Face your partner in a closed fighting stance. Kick at your partner using a pulling-step kick; rechamber your leg and set it down. Your partner does the same thing, kicking at you. Do this drill for one minute, then switch to a different kick without stopping. For example, begin with side kicks, switch to round kicks, and then switch to axe kicks. The focus is on quickly shifting your center of gravity, improving speed, balance, and timing in fast steps, front-foot round kicks, front-foot pushing kicks, front-foot side kicks, front-foot hook hicks, and front-foot axe kicks.

Kicking in a Circle

Side-step kicking in a circle will help you develop the ability to move laterally, improving agility, timing, and endurance.

This exercise uses simultaneous blocks and kicks. Face your partner. Begin in a natural stance. Slide the left foot to the right foot. As soon as the left foot touches the right foot, kick the right foot at your partner. Block your partner's kick with your left hand. All of this happens at the same time; both of you execute the same move. After you rechamber your leg and set down your right foot, take a pulling step to the right with the left foot, moving counterclockwise, and kick with the right foot. You should move in a circle. Repeat the exercise in a clockwise direction.

Blocking and Punching

These exercises will improve physical conditioning and eye–hand coordination as well as timing, agility, and endurance through simultaneous blocking and punching.

Stand in a natural stance facing your partner. Begin by blocking and punching at the same time while bounding in a counterclockwise circle. Begin slowly in order to get the pacing, than gradually increase the speed. Repeat the exercise in a clockwise direction.

10

Attacking

Attacking techniques can be classified as single direct attacks, multiple direct (combined) attacks, single indirect attacks, and multiple indirect attacks.

A single direct attack is used when the opponent shows no reaction or is about to attack at the position where the athlete is standing. The single direct attack is a preemptive, skillful attack. A multiple direct attack combines two or more movements. It also is a skillful attack, and it includes the fists.

A single indirect attack is a one-movement attack that combines steps or feinting motions. In a multiple indirect attack, the fighter attacks by combining two or more movements such as two steps or feints.

In a more general sense, attack techniques can be classified into seven categories:

1. Basic foot techniques
2. Attack techniques from the position where the athlete is standing, as in a counterkick
3. Attack and defense techniques by means of steps and feints
4. Grounded kicking techniques
5. Jump-kick techniques
6. Advanced kicking techniques
7. Techniques that combine hands and feet

Attack and defense techniques are as numerous as an athlete's imagination. An outstanding athlete can consider solutions to difficult situations as they happen during a match and execute skillful attacks or counterattacks. The majority of athletes, however, have a variety of techniques to use, but they fail to link those techniques to scoring moves.

It is essential for athletes to make accurate, fast attacks and counterattacks based on the instant evaluation of the opponent's moves and to link those techniques to scoring. In order to do this, athletes must master a few skills rather than try to be skillful at many techniques. It is essential to develop one or two special techniques that will enable you to carry out attacks and counterattacks faster than the opponent under any circumstances.

Even if a first attack or defense ends in failure, you should automatically link to a second attack or defense. The link to the second attack depends on your intention, but a third attack or continuous attack must be carried out automatically and without premeditation. For this reason, you need considerable practice with a variety of partners to learn to make the judgments that you will need in a real match.

In this chapter, we review various sparring styles that you may encounter in the ring and the attacking strategies for making the score. (Counterattacks are discussed in chapter 11.) First, each situation describes an opponent's method or style, followed by possible solutions. In some cases, multiple approaches may be suggested. The consummate athlete should have a repertoire of strategies. Only through practice and experience will these strategies become second nature.

SITUATION 1: TALL OR LARGE OPPONENT

If your opponent is very tall, it is necessary to adjust distance. Often a tall opponent has long legs. Athletes who keep their distance may lose their dominance in the match.

Hulking athletes are usually a little bit slower. Close into and move away from the opponent quickly. Combination attacks are best.

When the opponent attacks, attempt a cut kick combined with a feint motion to stop the forward motion. A cut kick coupled with a fast-step combined attack may give you the upper hand in the match. Also, in defense situations, the cut kick works in combination with a fist attack.

SITUATION 2: UNFAMILIAR OPPONENT

When you have no information on your opponent's style of fighting, you may want to use a variety of attacks and feints with the entire body or just the hands or feet in order to evaluate the opponent's reaction. If the opponent does not react, then try again by using a short cut kick or quick-step axe kick.

When attempting an attack, consider a rear-foot kick, spin back kick, or spin hook kick. If the opponent reacts with a spin back motion, then a good defense would be a cut kick of two movements by means of a feinting motion and an attack using the front foot. Pull the rear foot next to the front foot with a feint. Raise the front foot short and low with a cut-kick feint. Once more pull the rear foot forward and, at the same time, pull the cut kick up to stop a spin motion. The first cut kick is likely to miss the target when the opponent turns for a spin back kick or spin hook kick. A cut with two movements, one low and one high, with the same foot will create good timing and has a high probability of stopping the opponent's attack.

After restraining the attack with a quick combination and attacking with a double round kick, you might have the upper hand in the match.

SITUATION 3: ATTACK-ORIENTED OPPONENT

An attack-oriented opponent will attack first at the start of the match. When athletes specialize in offensive attacks, they will likely attack through combination moves. Their weakness may be counterattacks.

Once you know your opponent's tactics, a counterstrategy might be a front round kick to the face while maintaining position or a short axe kick to the face to disrupt forward momentum. Another strategy would be to sidestep the forward attack and counter from the off-center position.

SITUATION 4: HESITANT OPPONENT

Opponents who react to a rear round counterkick (counterkick reaction at position while hesitating with a nonaggressive stance) are probably unsure in their movements and hesitant to counterattack.

Check your opponent's reaction with a low, short cut kick or feinting motion. Let's say the opponent reacts in a slightly hesitant manner or backs off and shows a nonaggressive rear counterkick. Employ a first-strike strategy with a quick-step front cut kick. Follow through with the cut kick by raising the leg and pushing toward the opponent's trunk or groin. While pushing forward with the front foot, attack with a double round kick, fast-step round kick, or sliding round kick or running axe kick. Another option would be to take one long step forward, take a short jump with the front foot, and attack the opponent's face with a front-foot axe kick. These techniques will help you gain dominance in the match.

SITUATION 5: NONAGGRESSIVE OPPONENT

An opponent may react to a rear back kick by backing off in a nonaggressive stance. When an opponent displays a nonaggressive rear kick or backs off by steps and feinting motions when you attack, you need a rear round kick that is faster than the opponent's back kick. From a standard fighting stance of left foot forward, reverse your position. Launch the rear leg (left foot) as in a pushing kick to the opponent's waist or trunk and link it to a double round kick. It will then be possible to manage the match effectively.

SITUATION 6: LEFT-FOOTED OPPONENT

First, find out if the opponent is left-foot dominant by attacking with a rear round kick, left-foot counterkick, left-foot back kick, or front-foot attack. If the opponent has a nonaggressive attack and counterkick, don't change your stance. While in an open stance, use a front cut kick (left foot) and, at the same time, close in and attack with your fist and combine it with a foot attack. If your opponent attacks with a front cut kick and round kick, execute a front cut kick with a spin back kick using your right foot, making sure your timing is precise.

SITUATION 7: OPPONENT PULLS BACK

An opponent may pull back the front foot or back off by one step and counterkick. Evaluation indicates that the opponent reacts to a front-foot back kick when step and attack feints are used. The opponent waits for an attack with a nonaggressive stance.

To attempt an attack, keep some distance from the opponent. Feint an attack with one step forward on the rear (right) foot. At the same time, slide back at a 45-degree angle and then attack with the rear (left) foot. Timing is everything. The opening for this move occurs when the opponent's front foot touches the ground.

Or, from a starting stance, bring the rear (right) foot forward in an attack feinting motion. Land that foot where the left foot is, then swing the left foot to the rear to launch a combined attack.

SITUATION 8: OPPONENT SIDESTEPS AND REACTS

If the opponent reacts to the side when a feint attack is offered, a careful attack is required because the attack rhythm has been broken. Since it is not clear what kind of attack the opponent will make after sidestepping, you must evaluate the opponent's strategy through various feints. In this case, close in and keep your body blocked. Attempt a face attack with a kick or punch to the chest.

SITUATION 9: OPPONENT ATTACKS WEAKLY

When an opponent does not move from her position, cringes, or hesitates (showing that she is flustered or lacks adequate attack or defense techniques), or counters with a nonaggressive rear-foot round kick, she probably lacks confidence.

Use your whole body to make a variety of feinting motions. Bring the rear foot to the front, launch a short front-foot cut kick, and then slide back to position. Attempt to raise and lower the knee as if to axe kick and check your opponent's reaction. If your opponent is hesitant, she may not be ready for an attack. If that's the case, don't hesitate to attempt a bold attack with the fastest attack kick.

Sometimes the opponent does not move at all. This may imply that he is momentarily frozen due to lack of experience or he is waiting for an attack in order to counterattack. After deciphering the opponent's true intention as best you can, choose the proper technique and attempt an accurate and fast attack.

Attack 1

Attack with a front cut kick (low feint) followed by a round kick. With your left (front) foot, cut low and, without setting your foot down, execute a left round kick to the opponent's trunk or face (figure 10.1).

With your whole body, feint and check your opponent's reaction. If your opponent doesn't react to your feint, execute a short and low front-foot cut kick, using a pulling or slide step or skipping on the rear leg. Immediately follow the cut kick with a round kick to your opponent's face using the same leg.

If your opponent backs off slightly at your feint, pull your back foot toward your front foot and make a short feinting motion as if doing a low cut kick with your front foot. At the same time, raise the same foot high and connect to a round kick to the face. If your feint is slow or timed improperly, your opponent may attack you with a back kick or spin hook kick.

a

b

Figure 10.1 Opponent attacks weakly, attack 1: *(a)* cut low to gauge opponent's reaction; *(b)* follow with a round kick, taking your left foot to opponent's face.

Keep your center of gravity on your back foot while leaning your upper body back slightly and attacking your opponent's face.

Attack 2

Simultaneously block with your left hand and punch with your right. Follow with a round kick, taking your right rear foot to your opponent's ribs, trunk, or face (figure 10.2).

Use a whole-body feint to check your opponent's reaction. Your opponent may counterattack with a rear-foot round kick, making it necessary to block and punch at the same time—block with the left hand and punch with the right.

Figure 10.2　Opponent attacks weakly, attack 2. Round kick, taking right foot to opponent's trunk.

Follow with a rear-leg round kick to your opponent's trunk or face. Keep your weight on your front foot and your upper body slightly bent down while attacking with the kick.

When your opponent backs off, use a combination kick. Execute a round kick with your right foot to your opponent's trunk or ribs and a left-foot round kick to the face or execute a round kick with your right foot to your opponent's trunk or ribs and a back kick with your left foot to the trunk or face. Another option would be to execute a round kick combined with a spin back kick.

Attack 3

Use a long spin back kick, taking your right rear foot to your opponent's trunk or face (figure 10.3).

From your original position, execute a front-foot cut kick, alternating with a feinting motion. If your opponent does not show any reaction or is holding back, feint with a short and low front-foot attack and immediately execute a long spin back kick. If the back kick fails, you may be

a

Figure 10.3　Opponent attacks weakly, attack 3: *(a)* turn away from opponent, preparing for a long spin back kick.

(continued)

counterattacked. At the time of the attack, keep in mind the combination skill of punching and kicking in case you are countered.

After the attack, when you are close to your opponent, strike the trunk with your left fist and a crescent kick. If the back kick fails, attempt a front-foot hook kick to your opponent's face from the same position. When your opponent backs off, follow up with a combination attack such as a double round kick to your opponent's trunk or face.

b

Figure 10.3   Attack 3 *(continued): (b)* execute the spin back kick, taking the right foot to opponent's face.

Attack 4

Use a short axe kick, taking your rear (right) foot to your opponent's face (figure 10.4).

Use a whole-body feint to check your opponent's reaction. If your opponent hesitates in place and then reacts with a counterattack, cover and block with your left hand. At the same time, launch a short axe kick with your right (rear) foot. Raise your foot to the height of your opponent's face and strike downward. If your timing is off, your opponent may counterattack. If that's the case, consider punching with your left fist.

a   *b*

Figure 10.4   Opponent attacks weakly, attack 4: *(a)* lift knee in preparation for the kick; *(b)* execute a short axe kick with the right foot, aiming at opponent's face.

Shift your weight to your front foot when you attempt the attack. At the same time, your upper body should be bent forward slightly. When your opponent attacks after you make your attack, move in close and attempt a punching attack with a combination punch and kick.

Attack 5

Execute a fast round kick after a sliding or pulling step, taking your front (left) foot to your opponent's trunk or face (figure 10.5).

a　　　　　　　　　　　　　　　　　　　　　　　　　　　　　　*b*

Figure 10.5　Opponent attacks weakly, attack 5: *(a)* perform a sliding step; *(b)* execute a fast round kick, taking left foot to opponent's trunk.

By means of a feint, slide your back foot to your front foot. At the same time, check your opponent's reaction by alternately putting forward and rechambering a front axe cut kick with your left foot. If your opponent does not react, quickly execute a fast round kick to your opponent's trunk or face.

Quickly shift your weight from your front foot to your back foot when you attack. While kicking, lean your upper body backward slightly in order to improve your reach.

When your opponent is in place or closing in after your attack, punch the chest with your right fist or execute a crescent kick to the face. If your opponent backs off, try a combination attack such as a fast round kick, taking your front foot to your opponent's trunk, and a right round kick to the trunk or face; a double fast round kick followed by a round kick; or a fast round kick, taking your front foot to your opponent's trunk with a spin back kick to the trunk with your right foot.

Attack 6

Use a fast, short axe kick with a sliding or pulling step. Take your front (left) foot to your opponent's face (figure 10.6).

Check your opponent's reaction with a feint. Slide your whole body forward from your original position. If your opponent does not show any reaction

and stays in place, slide your back foot toward your front foot. At the same time, make a short jump with your front foot. Raise the bent knee up to chest height and strike down at your opponent's face with a short front axe kick.

Quickly shift your weight from your front foot to your back foot at the time of the attack. Keep your upper body bent forward slightly, using your abdominal muscles to raise your leg to your opponent's face. When your opponent backs off slightly, quickly attack with a round kick using either foot.

a

b

c

Figure 10.6 Opponent attacks weakly, attack 6: *(a)* perform a sliding step; *(b)* begin the kick; *(c)* execute a short axe kick with the left foot.

Attack 7

Execute a short double round kick. For the first kick, take your rear (right) foot to your opponent's trunk (figure 10.7a). On the second kick, take your left foot to the trunk or face (figure 10.7b).

a *b*

Figure 10.7 Opponent attacks weakly, attack 7: *(a)* on first kick of short double round kick, take right foot to opponent's trunk; *(b)* on second kick, take left foot to opponent's face.

Lightly jump in place and use your whole body to feint an attack. If your opponent doesn't react but hesitates, concentrate your power on your front (left) foot. With a feinting motion for attack, make a short and low kick with your rear (right) foot and make a short jump with your front (left) foot. Cross your feet in midair and attack with a double round kick.

If your opponent reacts by moving back, move forward and attempt a combination double round kick. The first attack is a feint; therefore it is inaccurate and it lacks power. The second attack is the main attack. Speed and timing are important.

Link the double round kick combination to a punch to the trunk with the fist and a spin back or spin hook kick. When backing off, attempt a combination attack such as a double round and spin back kick that takes your right foot to your opponent's trunk or face, or a spin hook kick and axe kick.

Attack 8

Execute a front short cut kick, feinting with your left foot, and then a spin hook or spin back kick, taking your right foot to your opponent's face (figure 10.8).

Check your opponent's reaction by raising or lowering your whole body in place. If your opponent hesitates and holds back, lift your front foot in a feint-

a

b

c

Figure 10.8 Opponent attacks weakly, attack 8: *(a)* feint with a front short cut kick; *(b)* turn away; *(c)* launch a spin back kick.

ing motion. At the same time, pull up your back foot slightly or skip forward. If your opponent backs off, attempt a spin hook kick to the face.

If the spin hook attack fails and your opponent counters with a rear-foot attack, defend yourself with a punching defense, a left-foot axe kick to the face, or a spin back kick to the trunk or face.

SITUATION 10: OPPONENT BACKS OFF OR REACTS BACK SLIGHTLY

When your opponent backs off, you have a unique opportunity to score. Sometimes while backing off, an opponent may try a back-foot counterattack. Check your opponent's reaction through diverse steps and feinting motions. If your opponent does not change stance and retreats either a short or long distance (i.e., backs off), she may show through body language that she is planning a counterattack. This is the moment to launch an attack. A fast kick is required. The five guidelines for such an attack are described in this section.

Figure 10.9 Opponent backs off or reacts back, attack 1. Move toward opponent with a pulling or sliding step, then attack with a fast round kick.

Attack 1

Use a pulling or sliding step and execute a fast round kick, taking your left foot to your opponent's trunk or face (figure 10.9).

After a fast or sliding step, launch a short front-foot axe kick through a feint, then move back. If your opponent moves back slightly and acts as if he will launch a rear-foot counterattack, slide your back foot up to your front foot and bend your front knee. Attack with an axe kick. The axe kick is executed as the opponent moves back. Lean your upper body backward slightly and make a long offensive kick.

The time to make a combination attack is when the opponent closes. Execute a punch to your opponent's trunk followed by a crescent or axe kick to the face.

If your opponent frequently moves back, use a fast round kick with your front (left) foot low or to your opponent's trunk and a round kick, taking your right foot to your opponent's trunk or face; or, use a fast round kick, taking your left foot to your opponent's trunk, and a spin back kick, taking your right foot to your opponent's trunk or face.

Attack 2

If your opponent reacts to a feint with a rear-leg attack, attack with an axe kick after a sliding or pulling step, taking your front (left) foot to your opponent's face.

With your whole body, feint a back-foot attack. If your opponent reacts with a rear-foot counterattack, slide or pull your rear foot toward your front foot. Jump slightly with your front foot and lift your bent front knee to chest height (figure 10.10). With your upper body slightly forward, execute an axe kick and then attack with a long axe kick while leaning back slightly.

If your opponent moves back, launch a combination attack such as a fast axe kick and double round kick or a fast axe kick and fast round kick.

Attack 3

If your opponent retreats by taking a long step back, try a running-step round kick, taking your left foot to your opponent's trunk or face (figure 10.11). Cross your feet in the air.

Move your rear foot one step forward and then return to your original place and feint. Usually your opponent

Figure 10.10 Opponent backs off or reacts back, attack 2. In preparation for the axe kick, raise your bent front knee to chest height.

will react by moving back. While moving your front (left) foot slightly back, quickly move your rear foot one step forward. Attack with a round kick using your front (left) foot while moving forward. If your opponent retreats with long steps, execute a double round kick after one step; a running round kick, taking your left foot to your opponent's trunk; and a round kick, taking your right foot to your opponent's trunk or face. Another option would be to execute a running step and a double round kick.

a   *b*

Figure 10.11   Opponent backs off or reacts back, attack 3: *(a)* opponent retreats with a long step back; *(b)* execute a running-step round kick, taking your left foot to your opponent's face.

Attack 4

If your opponent moves back, execute a short round kick, feinting with your right foot, and a double round kick with either foot.

Use a feinting motion to initiate a short round kick. When your opponent moves back, quickly attempt a combined attack using quick double round kicks. Lean forward for this attack. If your opponent closes in when you perform the double round kicks, use a combination fist attack and crescent kick to your opponent's face or a fist attack and short jump spin back kick or spin hook kick.

Attack 5

If your opponent retreats with a long step, execute a tornado kick, taking your left foot to your opponent's trunk or face.

While jumping lightly in place, feint with your whole body. Your opponent reacts by backing off. At this time, concentrate power to your front foot and, pivoting on that foot, rotate clockwise 180 degrees (figure 10.12a). Move your rear (right) foot one step forward. Make a short upward jump with your front (left) foot (figure 10.12b), cross your feet midair, and attack with your left foot (figure 10.12c). Lean the upper body backward slightly during the attack.

When your opponent moves back with long steps, attack with a tornado kick and spin back kick or spin hook kick as well as a tornado kick and round kick. The kicks can be performed with or without a slight jump.

a

Figure 10.12   Opponent backs off or reacts back, attack 5: *(a)* rotate clockwise 180 degrees.

(continued)

b

c

Figure 10.12   Attack 5 *(continued)*: *(b)* jump and cross feet in the air; *(c)* execute a tornado kick, taking your left foot to your opponent's trunk.

SITUATION 11: OPPONENT CHANGES STANCE

An opponent who changes stances (right foot to the front, left foot to the rear), backs off by one step and reverses the stance, or is left-foot dominant may be driven by one of these reasons:

- It is a habit.
- It is a strategy for creating a chance to attack.
- She is backing off so she can then counterattack.

Check the opponent with diverse steps and feinting motions to get a better sense of her motivation for changing her stance. It is necessary to find out whether this is just a habitual motion, if the opponent is left-foot dominant, or if the opponent reacts by getting ready for a left-foot back kick. There are seven suggested options for attacking this type of opponent.

Figure 10.13 Opponent changes stance, attack 1: Execute a round kick, taking your right foot to your opponent's trunk, while applying weight to your left foot.

a

Figure 10.14 Opponent changes stance, attack 2: *(a)* feint a front cut kick.

(continued)

Attack 1

When your opponent switches feet, execute a left-handed block and rear-foot round kick with your right foot to the trunk or face (figure 10.13). Lightly bound in place and then feint an attack with your whole body. The time to attack is when the opponent moves to switch feet in place. At that time, block with your left hand and attack with your rear (right) foot with a round kick while applying weight to your front (left) foot. When you attack, move your center of gravity to the front foot and lean the torso slightly forward. If the attack with a short kick fails, continue without interruption to a left-foot round kick.

Attack 2

When your opponent switches feet and form, feint a front cut kick with a rear round kick, taking your right foot to the trunk or face (figure 10.14). Make a feinting motion by lifting your front (left) foot short and low in place. Or, with a feinting motion, pull your rear (right) foot toward your front (left) foot while executing a front cut kick. In reaction, the opponent switches his stance either in place or backs off a step. At that moment, attack with a

b　　　　　　　　　　　　　*c*

Figure 10.14 Attack 2 *(continued): (b)* jump and switch feet in the air; *(c)* finish with a rear round kick, taking your right foot to your opponent's trunk.

quick rear-foot combination round kick. At the time of the attack, transfer your center of gravity from your rear (right) foot to your front foot. Execute a round kick with your torso leaning slightly forward.

If your opponent clinches when you attempt a front cut kick, immediately attack the chest with your fist or execute a crescent kick to the face in order to gain the advantage.

Attack 3

When your opponent takes one step back, try feinting a low, fast, front round kick with your left foot and follow up in the air with a round kick, taking your right foot to the trunk or face (figure 10.15). Jump (bound) lightly in place and then abruptly pull your rear (right) foot toward your front (left) foot. Start with a feinting attack and then attempt a long double round kick (right then left). This kick is initiated when the opponent backs off and

a

Figure 10.15 Opponent changes stance, attack 3: *(a)* feint a low front round kick with left foot.

(continued)

b   *c*

Figure 10.15   Attack 3 *(continued):* *(b)* jump in the air to switch feet; *(c)* finish with a round kick, right foot to opponent's face.

switches stances. At the time of the attack, lean your upper body backward slightly.

Attack 4

When the opponent takes one step back, try feinting a low front cut kick with your left foot, and then execute a spin back kick, taking your right foot to the trunk or face. When attacking, lift the front (left) foot in a fake cut motion. The opponent backs off one step and counters with a round kick using the foot that was taken back (figure 10.16).

Alternatively lift your front (left) foot and make a short cut kick. At the same time, pull your rear foot toward your front foot by a half step and make a long cut kick. Lean your upper body back slightly. Attempt an attack with a spin hook kick at the same time the opponent backs up one step and then begins to counter with a round kick.

Attack 5

If your opponent takes one step back, try a short rear round kick, feinting with the right foot, and a double round kick that takes your right foot to the trunk or face and your left foot to the trunk or face. Or, execute a triple round kick. Feint with the right and left legs and then take your right foot to the trunk or face.

Jump or bound lightly in place. Feinting a sudden attack, initiate a short rear round kick. Immediately follow up with a double round kick. Execute this motion as soon as your opponent retreats. Transfer your center of gravity

a

b

c

d

Figure 10.16 Opponent changes stance, attack 4: *(a)* feint with low front cut kick with left foot; *(b)* turn away to prepare for spin back kick; *(c)* opponent counters with a round kick; *(d)* finish with a spin back kick, taking your right foot to your opponent's face.

from your rear foot to your front foot. At the time of the double attack, lean your upper body forward slightly.

If your opponent clinches as soon as you initiate the cut kick, immediately execute a crescent kick to the face or punch the torso with your fist to create space. Add a short jump spin back or spin hook kick to the face.

If the opponent backs off very far at the time of the attack, the right spin back kick as a third attack is effective.

Attack 6

If your opponent takes one step back, take one step forward with the right foot and execute a double round kick with your left foot and then with your right foot to the trunk or face (figure 10.17).

a

b

c

Figure 10.17 Opponent changes stance, attack 6: (a) step forward with right foot; (b) with left foot, execute a round kick; (c) finish with a round kick, taking your right foot to your opponent's trunk.

When your opponent moves, take one step forward with your rear (right) foot to close the gap and lead off with a double round, left foot first.

Attack 7

If your opponent takes one step back, try a tornado double round kick. Take your left foot and then your right foot to your opponent's trunk or face.

Bound lightly in place. Suddenly fake an attack motion with a spin back kick. When your opponent tries to back off, pivot on your front (left) foot. Turn your rear (right) foot 180 degrees clockwise and move your front (left) foot one step forward. Lightly jump on your front (left) foot and cross your feet. Execute a double round kick, bringing your left foot and then your right foot to your opponent's torso or face. Lean your upper body back slightly and kick.

A lighter athlete may attack with a tornado double or triple jump round kick.

SITUATION 12: OPPONENT CLINCHES

A very aggressive opponent may show a tendency to clinch after you attack. These types of opponents also usually counterattack with their fists while clinching.

An opponent who is very aggressive and frequently clinches may be weak in counterattacking. When your opponent moves to attack with the rear (right) foot, don't take a full step back. Instead, move your front foot back about half a step and bend the left knee, lifting it to the level of your chest. Launch a short down axe kick to your opponent's face.

It may also be possible to bend the right knee in place and attempt a short down axe kick to your opponent's face or a pushing front kick to the chin.

When your opponent attacks with fists, counter with a short axe kick with either foot. When your opponent moves to attack with a double round kick (right then left foot), attack the face with a short jump spin back kick or spin hook kick.

When your opponent attacks with the front foot, stop the attack with an in-place front cut kick and initiate a short jump spin back kick or spin hook kick.

11

Counterattacking

In a direct counterkick attack, both fighters counterkick at the same time. In an indirect counterkick, one fighter steps aside or blocks the kick of the opponent and then counters with a kick.

A counterkick is a way to take control of the match by taking advantage of the opponent's weakness when she attacks. Counterkicks require precise reaction time and flexibility. Evaluate your opponent's movement instantly and kick automatically in reaction.

The counterkick demands quick judgment for good timing. For example, use feints to induce your opponent to attack. When your opponent attempts the attack, counterkick. Pay attention to your opponent's attack and counterattack techniques and use this information to exploit your opponent's weaknesses. Improve your ability to read and respond to your opponent through tactical training experience under realistic match conditions.

In this chapter we discuss counterstrategies to 11 different attacks. These strategies will help you build your repertoire of techniques in the ring. However, just reading about the counterattacks will not automatically create a good fighter. It will take much practice with different partners to make these motions second nature.

OPPONENT ATTACKS WITH A REAR ROUND KICK

The rear and front round kicks are two of the most frequently used scoring kicks. Rear and front round kicks create fast attacks and counterkicks at the same time. In addition, it is easy to link a rear round kick to a combination attack.

Use your judgment to read your opponent and deliver a quick counterattack. A combination of good timing and skill will give you control of the match.

Counterattack 1

When your opponent attempts to attack with a rear round kick, remain in place and block the kick with your left hand. At the same time, counter with a rear round kick (figure 11.1). This is a basic counter; you have to gain the advantage with good timing and good blocking. You have to be faster than your opponent.

a   *b*

Figure 11.1   Counterattacks to a rear round kick. Block opponent's kick with left hand and counter with a rear round kick *(a)* to the trunk or *(b)* to the face.

Counterattack 2

Another way to counterattack a rear round kick is to stay in place. Block low and lift your knee to your chest. When your opponent moves to attack you with the rear foot, shift your weight to your front foot and block with your left hand. At the same time, lift your rear knee to chest height and attack with a rear axe kick (figure 11.2). At the time of the attack, center your weight over your front foot and bend your trunk forward slightly. Depending on the situation, you may want to punch before kicking.

Counterattack 3

You can induce your opponent to attempt a rear round kick. When your opponent tries the rear round kick, counter with a short pulling-step front

a *b*

Figure 11.2 Counterattacks to a rear round kick. Block opponent's kick with left hand and counter with a rear axe kick *(a)* to the trunk or *(b)* to the face.

axe kick, taking your left foot to your opponent's face (figure 11.3). In order to induce a rear-foot (left-foot) attack, feint a rear-foot (right-foot) attack with your whole body. When your opponent moves to attack with the rear foot, bring your rear foot toward your front foot. Quickly shift your weight and bend your front foot. Lift it to chest height and attack your opponent's face with a short front axe kick. Drop your left arm to block the rear round kick. When moving forward, be sure to bend your trunk slightly forward and then lean backward slightly to attack.

Counterattack 4

When you induce your opponent to attack with a rear round kick, you can

Figure 11.3 Counterattacks to a rear round kick. Feint to entice opponent to attempt a rear round kick, block the kick with your left hand, and counter with a front axe kick to opponent's face.

also counter with a bada chagi (twist step). Using a feint, induce your opponent to attempt a rear-foot (right-foot) attack. Slide your whole body forward slightly and pull it back. When your opponent moves to attack with the rear (right) foot, block the opponent's round kick with your left hand. Shift your weight to the rear and bring your front (left) foot toward your rear foot with a twist step. Step to the side and simultaneously attack with your rear foot.

Figure 11.4   Counterattacks to a rear round kick. Counter with a twist step and a kick with the rear foot, leaning away from the kick.

Lean away from the kick (figure 11.4). If your opponent has a long rear kick, twist farther back to a 45-degree body position, sidestep, and attack at the same time.

Counterattack 5

When your opponent tries to attack with a rear round kick, another way to counterattack is by taking a sideways step with your right foot at a 45-degree angle. Plant your foot and then execute a rear round kick, taking your right foot to your opponent's trunk or face (figure 11.5). You can induce the attack from your opponent by feinting a short, low attack with a rear-foot (right-foot) round kick. Your opponent will move his rear foot to attack. When he does, lift your knee in a low, short motion as if kicking. Instead of kicking, plant your foot to the right side and shift your weight to the right. Slide your left foot toward your right foot when your opponent's kick drops forward. Shift your weight to your left foot and execute a round kick with your right foot with a slight rotating jump. Keep your body turned sideways. Alternatively,

a   *b*

Figure 11.5   Counterattacks to a rear round kick: *(a)* with right foot, step to the right at a 45-degree angle; *(b)* execute a rear round kick with right foot.

you could shift your weight from your front foot to your rear foot and attack when you step to the side. Lean slightly to the side and back as you kick. At close proximity, attacking your opponent's face with a crescent kick may also be effective. Another option would be to add another round kick to double the attack.

Counterattack 6

When your opponent attacks with a rear round kick with the right foot, block the kick with your left hand, punch your opponent in the trunk with your right hand, and then execute a round kick, taking your left foot to your opponent's trunk (figure 11.6). To induce your opponent to attack, move forward one step and feint a short rear-foot (right-foot) round kick. When your opponent uses the right foot to attempt a rear round kick, block the kick with your left hand. At the same time, punch with your right hand and initiate a clinch. Follow up with a round kick or crescent kick with your left foot to your opponent's face. Shift your weight slightly forward and bend your trunk forward slightly.

a   *b*

Figure 11.6 Counterattacks to a rear round kick: *(a)* block opponent's rear round kick with left hand and punch opponent's trunk with right hand; *(b)* perform a round kick with left foot to opponent's trunk.

Counterattack 7

Shuffle your feet back and execute a rear round kick with your right foot, aiming for your opponent's trunk or face. Apply power to your front foot and feint an attack with your entire body. When your opponent attacks with a rear round kick, shuffle back to avoid the kick. Counter with a round kick before your opponent's attacking foot touches the ground (figure 11.7).

a   **b**

Figure 11.7   Counterattacks to a rear round kick: *(a)* shuffle back to avoid opponent's rear round kick; *(b)* counter with a round kick to opponent's face.

Alternatively, apply power to your front foot and move your rear foot back first. Then step both feet backward. Keep your trunk bent back slightly and attack with your rear foot.

Counterattack 8

When your opponent attacks with a rear round kick using the right foot, shuffle back a little and execute a double round kick with your right foot to your opponent's trunk or your left foot to your opponent's trunk or face (figure 11.8).

a   **b**

Figure 11.8   Counterattacks to a rear round kick: *(a)* begin double round kick by taking right foot to opponent's trunk; *(b)* jump to rotate hips and switch feet.

(continued)

Slide your front foot forward slightly and feint an attack with a rear round kick motion. When your opponent attacks with the rear (right) foot, shuffle back slightly to avoid the kick. When your opponent's kick begins to drop forward, execute a short double round kick in place. Shift your weight to your front foot and attack. Keep your trunk bent back slightly. Remember to rotate your hips in the air.

c

Figure 11.8 Counterattacks to a rear round kick *(continued)*: *(c)* finish by taking left foot to opponent's face.

Counterattack 9

When your opponent attacks with a rear round kick, counterattack with a double round kick. Take your left foot to your opponent's trunk and your right foot to your opponent's trunk or face (figure 11.9).

When your opponent moves the rear (right) foot to attack, slide your front foot one step straight back. Plant your foot for a launch forward. Do not pivot on the right foot. As your opponent's foot drops forward after the round kick, attempt a short double round kick (left foot first) with or without a slight

a
b

Figure 11.9 Counterattacks to a rear round kick: *(a)* step back to avoid opponent's rear round kick; *(b)* begin short double round kick with left foot first.

(continued)

c

d

Figure 11.9   Counterattacks to a rear round kick *(continued): (c)* jump to rotate hips and switch feet; *(d)* finish the double round kick by taking your right foot to your opponent's trunk.

jump. Shift your weight to your front foot and bend your trunk forward slightly. Another option is a single left-foot rear round kick to the opponent's trunk or face.

Counterattack 10

When your opponent attacks with a rear round kick, counter with a spin back kick, taking your left foot to your opponent's trunk or face (figure 11.10).

a

b

Figure 11.10   Counterattacks to a rear round kick: *(a)* when opponent attacks with his right foot, begin a spin back kick with left foot; *(b)* take left foot to opponent's trunk.

Switch from an open to a closed stance to induce your opponent to attempt a rear-foot attack. As your opponent attacks with the rear (right) foot and before his foot lands, execute a rear-foot (left-foot) spin back kick or a spin hook kick to your opponent's trunk or face. Shift your weight to your front foot. When you spin, lean your trunk backward and make the attack.

Counterattack 11

When your opponent attacks with a rear round kick, counter with a spin hook kick, taking your right foot to your opponent's face (figure 11.11).

Time your counter to occur the moment your opponent moves his rear (right) foot for the rear round kick. Stay in place but shift your weight back to avoid the kick. As his kick begins to drop forward, spin your torso, look over your right shoulder, and execute a hook kick to your opponent's face. Bend at the waist to get height on the kick. You could also add a slight jump.

a

b

c

Figure 11.11   Counterattacks to a rear round kick: *(a)* shift back to avoid opponent's kick; *(b)* spin torso so back is to opponent; *(c)* execute a hook kick to opponent's face.

OPPONENT ATTACKS WITH A DOUBLE ROUND KICK

A double round kick consists of two motions: a feinting motion without power or accuracy and the main attack. It doesn't matter if the rear foot or front foot moves first. The target of a double round kick is the face or trunk.

The double round kick attack can come from the rear foot first or the front foot first with a fast forward motion and no interruption. The attack may come as a double with a third round kick thrown in without a jump. Therefore, a counterattack requires a fast read, good timing, and a decision to counter in place, shuffle back to get distance from the kick, or move in and clinch before the attack.

As your opponent moves forward, stop her momentum with a short front axe kick to the face or a rear kick to the trunk or face. You must use your best timing and all your flexibility. Another option is to shuffle backward as your opponent comes forward. As your opponent's kick lands, attack. The last option is to move in to clinch with a right punch to your opponent's chest followed by a front axe or spin back kick. Counter as your opponent comes forward.

Counterattack 1

When your opponent attempts a double round attack in place, counterattack with a front-foot short axe kick (left foot to opponent's face) or a pushing kick (left foot to opponent's chin) in place.

Check with a forward feinting motion. When your opponent moves the rear (right) foot to attack with a double round kick, shift your weight to your rear foot (figure 11.12a). Your center of gravity should be slightly backward

a   *b*

Figure 11.12 Counterattack to a double round kick: *(a)* when opponent moves his rear foot to begin his attack, shift weight to rear foot; *(b)* execute a short axe kick to opponent's face.

with a front-foot attack. Lift your knee to chest height and make a short, straight, light attack to your opponent's face to stop his momentum (figure 11.12b). A heavy attack isn't needed since your opponent's momentum will carry him into the bottom of your foot. The same technique can be used with a pushing kick with light contact to the face. Another option is to execute a rear foot axe kick or shuffle back as soon as the double attack begins, then perform a double round kick with the left foot to the trunk and the right foot to the trunk or face.

Counterattack 2

Counterattack a double round attack in place by trying to close to your opponent. Punch with your right hand to your opponent's trunk (figure 11.13) and execute a short jump spin back kick, taking your right foot to your opponent's trunk or face.

Figure 11.13 Counterattack to a double round kick. With right hand, punch to opponent's trunk.

Check forward with a feint to draw your opponent into attempting a kick. Time your counter to come at the moment when your opponent moves the rear (right) foot for the attack with a double round kick. Slide forward with your left foot and block with your left arm. Attack with a strong right punch to your opponent's trunk. The punch should displace your opponent enough for you to execute a short jump spin back kick with your right foot. Another option is to execute a short jump spin hook kick or a rear foot crescent kick to the opponent's face.

Counterattack 3

A double round attack can be executed with the front foot or rear foot leading. To counter, step with your rear foot at a 45-degree angle to the side (figure 11.14a) and then execute a rear-foot round kick, taking your right foot to your opponent's waist (figure 11.14b). Another option is to step to the side and perform a double round kick, taking your right foot to your opponent's trunk and your left foot to his trunk or face.

Check forward in a feint to induce your opponent to attempt a double round kick. Wait for the moment when your opponent moves her rear (right) foot to attempt a double round kick. As your opponent begins the first kick, slide your right foot to the side, away from your opponent's forward motion. As your opponent lands the second kick on the ground, move your left foot to join your right foot and then quickly execute a kick with your right leg to

a   b

Figure 11.14 Counterattack to a double round kick: *(a)* step away from opponent when he attempts the round kick; *(b)* execute a round kick, taking your right foot to your opponent's waist.

your opponent's back side. Note that when you step to the side, you keep your body weight over your right foot. As you kick with your right foot, lean back slightly and rotate your body to the right.

This strategy will also work if your opponent leads off with a front-foot double round. Your movements will be the same either way.

Counterattack 4

The double round attack can be executed in place or with a shuffle forward. To counter, execute a jump spin back kick in place or shuffle back and back kick in place, targeting your opponent's trunk or face.

Time your counter to occur the moment your opponent moves the rear (right) foot for the double round kick. The best method is to attack your opponent's trunk or face with a short jump spin back kick in place at the moment your opponent moves the rear foot. Speed and timing are required although the jump is optional. If your opponent is quick and has already started the first kick, you should shuffle back to gain distance. As your opponent begins the second kick, execute a short jump spin back kick. If your opponent's double attack covers a larger distance, take a long shuffle step back and counter with a jump spin back kick or hook kick.

Counterattack 5

An attack with a double round kick can be countered by taking one step back with the front (left) foot, either straight back or at a 45-degree angle, and attacking with a round kick, taking the rear (left) foot to your opponent's trunk or face.

When your opponent moves the rear (right) foot to execute the double round kick, shuffle back one long step with your front (left) foot (figure 11.15). Wait until your opponent finishes the attack (both kicks) and both feet are on the ground again, then apply power to your rear (left) foot and push forward for a left-foot round kick.

Alternatively, you can step back with your front (left) foot at a 45-degree angle to the left. Pull your right foot to your rear foot, twist your torso, and kick with the left foot. Which method to use

Figure 11.15 Counterattack to a double round kick. Shuffle back at a 45-degree angle and wait for your opponent to finish attacking.

depends on your distance to your opponent. The twist step is more of an in-place attack. Another option is, after taking one step back, launch a spin back kick or spin hook kick.

Counterattack 6

A double round attack can be executed with the front or rear foot. Counter by sliding backward one long step with both feet or taking a fast step back and executing a double round kick. When done correctly, both feet slide along the floor. Take your right foot to your opponent's ribs and your left foot to the trunk or face.

Execute a front cut-step kick and rechamber your leg in a feinting motion. When your opponent moves the rear (right) foot for the double round kick, shuffle back one step. When your opponent's feet touch the ground after the attack, immediately execute a short double round kick (right foot, then left foot). Shift your body weight to your front foot and lean your trunk forward slightly. Sprint forward in short steps and attack with kicks. Another option is to shuffle back to avoid the first round kick and immediately, before the second kick, attack with a rear round kick to the opponent's trunk or face.

Counterattack 7

With your front foot, turn 180 degrees to the back, pivot both feet forward, and shuffle back. Execute a round kick in place or with a jump, taking your left foot to your opponent's trunk or face (reverse tornado).

Wait until your opponent moves the rear (right) foot for the double round kick. Pivot on your rear (right) foot, turn your front (left) foot 180 degrees clockwise, and shuffle back. With the front foot, make a short jump and attack with a left-foot round kick. Time your counter to come when your opponent's attack ends and both feet touch the ground (figure 11.16).

If your opponent is executing a fast double round kick (front foot first), shuffle back one long step. As the second kick begins to drop, immediately attack with a rear round kick (right foot) or use a twist step and a rear round kick.

a   *b*

Figure 11.16   Counterattack to a double round kick: *(a)* wait until opponent's feet are on the ground again before launching counterattack; *(b)* execute a round kick, taking your left foot to your opponent's face.

OPPONENT ATTACKS WITH A FAST KICK

In this section, we review counterstrategies for attacks that feature a fast kick and pulling-step round kick or a running-step round kick. Fast kicks—front-foot round, axe, and pushing kicks—are used in a high percentage of attacks and are usually good scoring kicks; therefore, it is important to have a strategy to counteract these kicks.

Counterattack strategy centers on feints, timing, distance, and front-foot attacks. Usually the attack sequence is made up of two motions; for example, the attacker executes a fast kick, slides the rear leg to the front foot, and immediately kicks with the front foot. In a running-step round kick, the rear leg quickly crosses the front foot and the kick is executed immediately.

As your opponent moves to attack and brings the rear leg forward, you should be ready to move as soon as the second motion starts or when the second motion is finished. If your timing is off and you miss the first motion, you should clinch, step to the side, or move back until your opponent finishes the second motion before attacking.

Counterattack 1

In the first situation, your opponent attacks with a pulling step followed by a fast kick and a front round kick with the left foot. Counter with an axe kick in place, with the option of executing a front round kick.

As your opponent brings the rear leg forward to the front foot or as she motions forward with her body, use this opening to shift your weight back and prepare for the counter. As your opponent begins her second motion, you should have your knee to your chest, ready to strike at the same time (figure 11.17). Strike your opponent lightly in the face to stop her momentum. Your opponent's forward momentum will increase the impact of the strike. As you raise your knee, lean forward with your upper body. Lean back slightly as you deliver the axe kick.

Figure 11.17 Counterattack to a fast kick. When opponent begins second motion, have knee to chest, ready for kick.

Counterattack 2

In the second situation, your opponent attacks with a fast, pulling, or running step forward followed by a front round kick. Counter by shuffling back with both feet in a fast step and executing a front round kick to your opponent's trunk or face.

As your opponent brings the rear leg toward the front foot or as he motions forward with his body, use the opening to shuffle back. Stand with your front knee slightly bent (cat stance; figure 11.18) and your leg ready to

Figure 11.18 Counterattack to a fast kick. The cat stance will prepare you for the counterkick.

counter with a round kick. Center your weight to start and then shift slightly back for the round kick. As your opponent's leg is at full extension or dropping, strike with a round kick. You may need to skip forward to close the gap. You can also time your counter so that you execute it when your opponent starts to move. Additionally, you can link a second kick—such as a round, axe, or crescent kick—to the round kick in combination.

Counterattack 3

An attack in which your opponent executes a fast, pulling, or running step followed by a front round kick can be countered with a spin hook kick or a jump spin hook kick that takes your right foot to your opponent's face.

As your opponent moves forward to begin a pulling step, read those motions to time your next move. Time your kick to begin as your opponent is midway through the pulling step. As your opponent begins the second motion, shuffle back to avoid the kick. As his kick begins to drop forward (figure 11.19a), pivot and execute a spin hook kick to his face (figure 11.19b). Another option is a jump spin back kick in place.

a   b

Figure 11.19 Counterattack to a fast kick: (a) pivot as opponent's kick drops forward; (b) follow with a spin hook kick to opponent's face.

Counterattack 4

For the next counterattack, take one step back with both feet and execute a double round kick, taking your right foot to your opponent's trunk (figure 11.20a) and your left foot to your opponent's face (figure 11.20b). This strategy counters an opponent who executes a front round kick after taking a fast, pulling, or running step forward.

Bound in place while waiting for your opponent to attack. Use a fake motion to draw in your opponent for the kick. Shuffle back in a reverse fast step and

a *b*

Figure 11.20   Counterattack to a fast kick: *(a)* for the first kick of a double round kick, take right foot to opponent's trunk; *(b)* for the second kick, take left foot to opponent's face.

hesitate as your opponent executes a round kick and starts to rechamber the leg. As your opponent's foot starts to land, execute a double round kick with or without a jump, right foot first. Another option is a fast step back and a single round kick with the rear (right) foot to the opponent's trunk or face.

When shuffling back, shift your weight to your front foot and lean slightly forward so that you are ready to launch the rear-leg round kick. Remember to rotate the hips in the air. The first kick of the double round is short and more of a fake. The second kick is the scoring kick.

Counterattack 5

The next counterattack uses a tornado kick to the opponent's trunk or face after a step back. This counters a front round kick following a fast, pulling, or running step from your opponent.

Fake forward, maybe more than once, to draw your opponent in for the attack. Shuffle back a little or a lot, depending on your opponent's initial forward motion. As your opponent begins to lift the leg for the round kick, pivot clockwise to set up for a full rotation. As your opponent's leg lands, you should be fully rotated. Execute a jump round tornado kick. Another option is a single round kick with the left foot to the opponent's face or a reverse tornado kick.

Counterattack 6

Again, your opponent is attacking with a front round kick following a fast, pulling, or running step forward. Take one step straight back or at a 45-degree angle to the side with your front foot and execute a round kick with your left foot, targeting your opponent's trunk or face.

Bound in place and fake a motion forward by sliding on your front foot and moving your body weight forward. If your opponent reacts by beginning his first motion with his feet together or across in a running step, move your foot straight back without pivoting on the front foot or move it to the side at a 45-degree angle. Shift your body weight to the side. As your opponent makes his second motion, either beginning the round kick or starting to drop his leg, launch forward off your rear (left) foot from the back or side to execute a round kick to the opponent's trunk or face. Another option is a double round kick, taking the right foot to the trunk or face and the left foot to the face, or a rear axe kick, taking the left foot to the face.

If you plant your left foot to the rear, do not change your body stance. The trunk is still forward and the left foot is straight back with the toes bent and touching the floor to push forward for the round kick. If you plant your left foot to the side, lean in that direction before executing the kick.

Figure 11.21   Counterattack to a fast kick. Clinch and punch opponent's chest before executing a spin hook kick.

Counterattack 7

In this counterattack to a front round kick following a fast, pulling, or running step forward, you will clinch while punching your opponent's chest (figure 11.21) and executing a spin hook kick.

Bound in place and read your opponent before she starts to move. As your opponent initiates her attack, move forward by sliding on your front foot and bringing your rear foot to join it. At the same time, block your opponent's front round kick with your right hand. With your left hand, punch your opponent's chest. During this move, you must also shift your body clockwise so as to minimize the impact of the blocked kick. As your opponent finishes the round kick, execute a short jump spin back kick.

In this case, your punch is not necessarily a scoring punch by virtue of impact. More importantly, it is a way to position your opponent for your jump spin back kick. Other options after the block and punch besides the jump spin kick are a double round kick, scissor step with a rear round kick, jump spin back kick, rear crescent kick, or rear round kick.

OPPONENT ATTACKS WITH AN AXE KICK

As an attack, the hop-step jump axe kick can be done in a couple of ways. For a short distance, the feet come together and the knee is raised to launch the axe kick. If more distance needs to be covered, then a step forward may be taken before jumping for the axe kick. Your opponent might even link a second kick to the jump axe kick. These are important differences to note when planning a counterattack.

It is necessary to consider the distance when planning your counter to an axe kick. The opportunity for the counterattack comes when your opponent's axe kick is in the air or the foot is coming down. You can use a variety of fake motions to draw your opponent in for the kick.

Counterattack 1

The opponent attacks with a front-foot axe kick, fast axe kick, or pulling-step axe kick. To counter, take a short jump in place and execute a spin back kick or spin hook kick.

Bound or fake to draw in your opponent. When your opponent starts the initial move for the jump axe kick, watch his forward motion for your chance to jump. As soon as your opponent brings his right foot forward to start the jump axe kick, immediately spin your torso (figure 11.22) and execute a jump spin back kick. If your opponent moves in too quickly and you miss the chance to jump spin, shuffle back and immediately kick as your opponent's axe kick is in the air or his leg is beginning to drop.

Figure 11.22 Counterattack to an axe kick. As opponent's leg starts to drop, spin and jump for a jump spin back kick.

Counterattack 2

Your opponent attacks with a front-foot axe kick, fast axe kick, or pulling-step axe kick. To counterattack, take one fast or long shuffle step back with both feet and execute a front-foot round kick, taking your left foot to your opponent's trunk or face.

Bound and fake forward to draw in your opponent. As soon as your opponent's body starts the forward motion but the feet are not yet together, shuffle back to a cat stance with your left leg bent, ready to kick. Your opponent executes the hop-step axe kick. Counterkick with your front foot when your opponent's leg is in the air or on its way down.

If you wait until your opponent brings the right foot forward and his body is in motion for the hop-step axe kick, your counterkick will be too late. You must execute the kick at the right moment. When executing the round kick, make sure your body is angled away from your opponent's axe kick. Lean back and extend the leg for the round kick. Another option is to take a short shuffle step forward with a front axe kick to your opponent's face or a fast round kick to his trunk or face.

Counterattack 3

Your opponent attacks with a front-foot axe kick, fast axe kick, or pulling-step axe kick. Counterattack by taking both feet back at the same time and executing a double round kick. Take your right foot to your opponent's trunk and your left foot to the trunk or face.

Bound or check to draw in your opponent. As soon as your opponent pulls his rear foot across to his front, shuffle back with both feet to avoid the kick. Wait for your opponent to finish the kick. When your opponent's kick is starting to drop, move in with a double round kick, with or without a jump, using the right leg first. On the first kick, target your opponent's backside ribs (figure 11.23a). This is not really the scoring kick; take the second kick to your opponent's trunk or face for the score (figure 11.23b). Remember to rotate your hips in the air.

This counter is all about waiting for the right moment. If the double round counterkick is executed too soon, you will get hit by your opponent's axe kick.

a *b*

Figure 11.23 Counterattack to an axe kick: *(a)* the first kick targets the opponent's backside ribs; *(b)* the second kick is the scoring kick, targeting the opponent's face.

As your opponent's leg is almost to the floor, move in with the double round kick. Another option is to execute a fast step back and a rear round kick; a fast front round kick, taking your left foot to your opponent's trunk or face; or a short hop step with a front axe kick.

Counterattack 4

Your opponent attacks with a front-foot axe kick, fast axe kick, or pulling-step axe kick. Counter by taking one step back with your front foot and executing a round kick, taking your left foot to your opponent's trunk or face. You could also step back and 45 degrees to the left with your front foot.

Bound in place and fake a motion forward by sliding on your front foot and moving your body weight forward (figure 11.24). If your opponent reacts by bringing her feet together or crossing her feet in a running step, either move your front foot straight back without pivoting on it or move it to the side at a 45-degree angle, shifting your body weight to the side to avoid the kick. As your opponent makes her second motion, beginning the axe kick, or as she starts to drop her leg, launch forward off your rear (left) foot from the back or side to execute a round kick. Even if you plant your left foot to the rear, do not change your stance. Keep the trunk forward and take the left foot straight back with the toes bent and touching the floor to push forward for the round kick. If you plant your left foot to the side, lean your body weight in that direction before you execute the round kick. A double round kick or a rear axe kick are also options.

Figure 11.24 Counterattack to an axe kick. Move front foot straight back and launch a round kick off the rear foot.

Counterattack 5

Your opponent attacks with a long front-foot axe kick, fast axe kick, or pulling-step axe kick. Counter by shuffling back one step and performing a tornado kick.

Figure 11.25   Counterattack to an axe kick. Take a long shuffle step back to avoid opponent's long kick.

Shuffle a long step back to avoid the kick if your opponent moves forward with a long reach (figure 11.25). When your opponent brings the feet together to initiate the hop-step axe kick, pivot clockwise in preparation for full rotation. As your opponent's foot comes down from the axe kick, fully rotate back to the front. Execute a fake with your right leg and perform a left round kick as the scoring kick. You also have the option to link another kick such as a round kick, with or without a jump, to the tornado kick.

OPPONENT ATTACKS WITH A CUT KICK OR PUSHING KICK

When an opponent attacks with a front-foot cut kick or pushing kick aimed at the trunk or hip, the cut or pushing kick is used to create an opening for a second scoring motion. As a counterattack, the cut or pushing kick is also used to stop the opponent's forward motion. If the attacker comes at you with a cut or pushing kick, your strategy is to avoid the first motion and then counterattack.

Counterattack 1

Your opponent attacks with a front-foot cut or pushing kick, aiming at your trunk or face. Counter with a cut or pushing kick. Try to close the gap at the same time. Use your left hand to block and your right hand to punch. Execute a jump spin hook kick, taking your right foot to your opponent's trunk or face.

As your opponent moves in with the hop front cut kick, pull your rear foot to the front and react forward with a clinch while blocking your opponent's left leg with your left hand and using your right hand to punch your opponent's ribs. The punch creates some distance before you execute the kick. Spin around and perform a spin hook kick, with or without a jump, taking your right foot to your opponent's face. Other options are a rear foot crescent kick, rear foot round kick, or double round kick.

Counterattack 2

Your opponent attacks with a cut or running step rear pushing kick. At the same time, counter with a spin back kick, jump spin back kick, or jump spin hook kick, taking your right foot to your opponent's trunk or face (figure 11.26).

Figure 11.26 Counterattack to a cut kick or pushing kick with an in-place jump spin back kick.

Fake and draw in your opponent. Before your opponent gets the cut kick in, when the feet come together or cross over for a running cut kick, jump around for a spin hook kick—no waiting. Lean your upper body forward on the rotation to get extension for the back kick.

Counterattack 3

Your opponent attacks with a fast front cut or front pushing kick. Counter by taking one step back with your front foot or stepping back at a 45-degree angle and performing a round kick, taking your left foot to your opponent's trunk or face (figure 11.27).

Figure 11.27 Counterattack to a cut kick or pushing kick. Perform a round kick with your left foot, targeting your opponent's face.

Bound in place and make a fake motion forward. If your opponent reacts with a first motion, move your foot straight back without pivoting on the front foot or move your foot to the side at a 45-degree angle and shift your body weight to the side. As your opponent makes the second motion (the cut is fully forward or the leg is starting to rechamber from a pushing kick), launch forward off the rear (left) foot from the back or side to execute a rear round kick to your opponent's trunk or face.

If you plant your left foot to the rear, do not change your stance. Keep your trunk forward and left foot straight back with toes bent and touching the floor to push forward for the round kick. If you plant your left foot to the side, lean in that direction before executing the rear round kick with your left foot. An alternative kick is a double round kick (with or without a jump), taking your left foot to your opponent's trunk and your right foot to his trunk or face.

Counterattack 4

Your opponent attacks with a fast front cut, running-step rear cut, or pushing kick. Counter at the same time with a cut kick, pulling your rear foot to the front and performing a hop cut kick. Don't drop the kick or rechamber but immediately lift it to a round kick to the face. Another option: after the initial cut, punch with your right fist to your opponent's trunk, then launch a rear crescent kick or spin hook kick to the face.

Counterattack 5

Your opponent attacks with a fast front cut kick, running rear-foot cut kick, or pushing kick. Counterattack by stepping your rear (right) foot to the right 45 degrees and executing a right round kick to your opponent's trunk or face.

Before stepping to the side, bring your right foot forward as if you are stepping forward. Do not plant your foot but move it to the side and launch a rear round kick. Wait for your opponent's kick to begin to drop before executing your round kick.

Figure 11.28 Counterattack to a cut kick or pushing kick. With your right hand, block your opponent's rear kick. With your left hand, punch him in the trunk. Follow with a short jump spin back kick or hook kick.

Counterattack 6

Your opponent attacks with a fast front cut kick, running rear-foot cut kick, or pushing kick. Counter with a block and a punch and a short jump spin back kick.

As your opponent's rear foot moves toward the front foot for the cut kick, your rear foot should be swinging clockwise past your forward position. Turn your torso to the closed position. Block your opponent's rear kick with your right hand, punch his trunk with your left hand (figure 11.28), and immediately pivot into a short jump spin back kick or hook kick.

Alternatively, after your opponent moves forward for the cut kick, step back clockwise to a closed position and launch a double round kick, with or without a jump, taking your right foot to his trunk and your left foot to his trunk or face.

OPPONENT ATTACKS WITH A TORNADO KICK

When your opponent strikes with a tornado kick, the best moment to counter is during the initial phase of the opponent's rotation. Tornado kicks are used to confuse and surprise the opponent. If the tornado kick is not executed quickly, you will have a better chance to time your counterattack. The counterattack to a tornado kick is all about timing.

Counterattack 1

Your opponent attacks with a tornado kick. Counterattack in place with a round kick using your rear foot, taking your foot to your opponent's trunk or face.

As soon as your opponent begins the motion for the tornado kick, look for him to rotate his upper body. When he does, shift your weight forward (figure 11.29a). As your opponent comes around, launch a rear leg round kick to the trunk or face since your opponent will be in an open stance (figure 11.29b). If he is in anything other than an open stance, you have missed your opportunity. Lean back to avoid the tornado kick and fully extend your leg for the round kick. For another option, you can double this kick with another kick, taking your left foot to your opponent's trunk or face.

a *b*

Figure 11.29 Counterattack for a tornado kick: *(a)* when opponent rotates his torso, shift your weight forward; *(b)* as your opponent comes around, execute a rear leg round kick to your opponent's torso.

Counterattack 2

Your opponent attacks with a tornado kick. Counter with a short jump spin back kick, taking your right foot to your opponent's trunk or face. You can execute the kick while standing in place or after shuffling back with both feet.

Watch for your opponent to rotate almost all the way around. When the leg starts to come up for the tornado kick, depending on the distance between you and your opponent, you should either shuffle back slightly or remain in position and execute a short jump spin back kick. Your opponent's body should be in a more forward-facing position in the tornado sequence. Center your weight and stand in a slight squat in order to jump for the back kick. Execute the kick simultaneously with your opponent's rotation.

Counterattack 3

Your opponent attacks with a tornado kick. Counter with a short spin hook kick, taking your right foot to your opponent's face. You can perform the kick while staying in place or you can shuffle back with both feet before launching the kick.

Watch for your opponent to rotate almost all the way around. When the leg starts to come up for the tornado kick, either shuffle back slightly or stay in place (depending on distance) and execute a short jump spin hook kick to your opponent's face. Your opponent's body should be in a more forward-facing position in the tornado sequence. Center your weight and stand in a slight squat in order to jump for the hook kick. Your opponent's body rotation and your kick are executed simultaneously.

Counterattack 4

Your opponent attacks with a tornado kick either in place or after pulling his rear foot to his front foot. Counter with either a hop-step front cut kick and double round kick or a front pushing kick and double kick. The target for the front cut kick and the front pushing kick is your opponent's side. For the double round kick, take your left foot to your opponent's trunk and your right foot to the face.

Fake with your front foot in a hop-step cut kick. You might have to do it more than once to draw in your opponent. When your opponent's upper body twists for the rotation, kick to the ribs or trunk using a rear- or front-leg cut kick. The cut kick will put your opponent off balance (figure 11.30). Use the cut kick as the launch for a single or double round kick.

The cut kick has to be accurate. If the cut kick is delivered too far to the left, your opponent's rotation may cause you to push through. The cut kick has to catch right outside of your opponent in order to stop the rotation and forward motion. When using the cut kick, shift your body weight to your rear foot, slide your rear foot to the front foot, and lean your upper body forward to create momentum.

Figure 11.30 Counterattack for a tornado kick. Use a cut kick to your opponent's side to knock him off balance.

Counterattack 5

Your opponent attacks with a tornado kick. Counter with a round kick, taking your left foot to your opponent's trunk or face. Before the kick, step at a 45-degree angle to the left with your front (left) foot.

When your opponent twists the upper body for the rotation, take one step at a 45-degree angle back with the left foot. When your opponent comes fully around for the tornado kick and the foot starts to drop, come back with a rear round kick (left foot) to the trunk or face. You can pull the right to the left with or without a slight jump. Remember to rotate the hips. Another option is to double the round kick with a second kick, taking your right foot to your opponent's trunk or face.

Counterattack 6

Your opponent attacks with a tornado kick. Counter by stepping back with both feet and launching a double round kick. Take your right foot to your opponent's trunk or ribs and your left foot to the trunk or face.

Shuffle back with both feet as your opponent begins to turn. When your opponent executes the tornado kick and the foot begins to drop, come forward with a double round kick. Take your rear (right) leg to the trunk and then take the second kick to the trunk or face. Your body weight should be moving forward.

Counterattack 7

Your opponent attacks with a tornado kick. Try to close the gap. Block the kick with your right hand, punch with your left hand, and execute a short jump spin back kick, taking your right foot to your opponent's trunk or face.

As your opponent rotates, move forward in a clinch using a right-handed block and left-handed punch. The forward movement can be slightly to the left side. Turn 180 degrees and lean forward and then jump for the back kick. The punch is not for scoring but rather to stop your opponent. Alternatively you can execute a spin hook kick from where you stand or shuffle back slightly or you can attempt an axe kick after the block and punch.

Counterattack 8

Your opponent attacks with a tornado kick. Counter with a reverse tornado kick with or without a jump.

As your opponent begins to rotate for the tornado kick, turn 180 degrees clockwise by stepping to the rear (figure 11.31a). Your front foot will pass your right ankle on the outside. This will help you avoid the round kick (figure 11.31b). As your opponent's kick begins to drop, immediately turn forward, completing the full circle, and launch a rear round kick to his trunk or face (figure 11.31c). Alternatively, hold your left foot in the air and kick with your right foot. You will need to rotate your hips to do this.

a

Figure 11.31   Counterattack for a tornado kick: *(a)* turn clockwise, stepping to the rear.

(continued)

b

b   *c*

Figure 11.31 Counterattack for a tornado kick *(continued)*: *(b)* continue to move in a circle, avoiding your opponent's kick; *(c)* execute a rear round kick to your opponent's trunk.

OPPONENT ATTACKS WITH A REAR-FOOT AXE KICK

Since head shots earn 2 points under the current rules, the axe kick has become a favorite attack; therefore, it is crucial to be able to counter this strategy. Various faking motions and steps can be used to induce the axe kick so that a successful countermotion can nullify the 2 points.

Counterattack 1

Your opponent attacks with a rear-foot axe kick. Twist your front foot toward your rear foot and execute a round kick, taking your right foot to your opponent's trunk or face.

When your opponent begins to move forward, shift your weight to your back foot. When your opponent's axe kick is high, swing your front (left) foot back counterclockwise and to the outside with a slight jump. Rotate the hips. With your rear (right) foot, deliver a round kick to your opponent's trunk or face. Your footwork should be simultaneous—when your front foot swings back, raise your rear foot for the round kick. Lean your upper body backward so you don't get hit by your opponent's axe kick.

Counterattack 2

Your opponent attacks with an axe kick using the rear foot. To counter, step back slightly with both feet and execute a round kick, taking your right foot to your opponent's trunk or face (figure 11.32).

a   b

Figure 11.32   Counterattack for a rear-foot axe kick: *(a)* step back to avoid opponent's kick; *(b)* counter with a round kick to opponent's face.

As your opponent moves forward, shuffle back on both feet. To shuffle back, you can move both feet together, slide the right foot first and follow with the left foot, or slide the left foot first and then follow with the right foot. When your opponent's kick is at full height and just starting to drop, deliver a rear round kick with your right foot. Shift your weight forward on your left foot in order to provide forward power for the rear round kick. Another option is to punch your opponent's trunk with your right hand and follow with the rear-leg round kick. Alternatively execute a double round kick as the second kick, taking your left foot to your opponent's trunk or face.

Figure 11.33   Counterattack for a rear-foot axe kick. Step back and lean away from the kick.

Counterattack 3

Your opponent attacks with an axe kick using the rear foot. Take your front foot straight back without pivoting on the right foot and execute a double round kick. Take your left foot to your opponent's trunk and your right foot to the trunk or face.

As your opponent moves forward, step straight back, leaning away from the kick (figure 11.33). When your opponent's kick is at full height and starts to drop, deliver a round kick, starting with the rear (left) foot. The first kick is more of a fake than a scoring kick. The second round kick should be to the trunk or face. Depending on the distance between you and your opponent, a triple round kick might give you more forward motion. After stepping back, another option is a spin into a hook kick instead of a double round kick. Make it a single kick.

Counterattack 4

Your opponent attacks with an axe kick, using the rear foot. Counterattack with a spin hook kick in place, taking your left foot to your opponent's face.

When your opponent moves in with the rear-foot axe kick, wait for the downward movement of the kick. As your opponent's foot heads for the floor, execute a spin hook kick to the face. This technique works only if your timing is right. You don't really move; you deliver the hook kick from your starting stance but lean back to avoid your opponent's kick. If your timing is off, you may need to switch your stance, wait, and then deliver the spin hook to the opposite (open) side. Switching the stance can also be used as a fake to draw in your opponent for the attack.

Counterattack 5

Your opponent attacks with a rear-foot axe kick. With your right foot, step at a 45-degree angle to the side and counter with a round kick, taking your right foot to your opponent's trunk or face.

As your opponent moves forward, move your rear foot to the side or slightly back and to the side in order to get out of the way. Part of this move is a faking motion. The rear foot can come off the ground in a forward movement, maybe more than once. If your opponent takes the bait, move your right foot to the side. Then as your opponent's kick starts to drop, slide your left foot to the position of the right foot and execute a round kick with your right foot. Center your body weight. Shift forward for the fake and lean toward your supporting foot before the kick. Lean back slightly to deliver the kick. As an option, you could connect a round kick with your left foot to make it a double kick.

Counterattack 6

Your opponent attacks with a rear-foot axe kick. Counter with a jump back kick.

You can use a variety of fakes to draw in your opponent. You must watch your opponent's movements to determine the timing of the footwork. As your opponent moves forward, step off at a 45-degree angle to the side with your rear foot. When your opponent's foot starts to drop, slide your left foot back toward your right foot and immediately rotate clockwise to deliver a jump spin back kick to your opponent's trunk or face, with or without a jump. A spin hook kick is another option.

OPPONENT ATTACKS WITH A SPIN BACK KICK

A high percentage of counterattacks fall under the category of the spin back kick. Spin back kicks can be used as an attack strategy, but the execution must be fast to be successful. If the opponent is known to use spin back kicks as a counter, it may be necessary for you to induce the spin back kick by feinting.

Counterattack 1

Your opponent attacks with a spin back kick. Counter the attack with a right-foot round kick to the trunk or face. Twist your front foot and step back at a 45-degree angle to the right.

Stand in ready stance and fake to draw in your opponent for an attack. As soon as your opponent begins the upper-body motion that signals the beginning of the spin back kick, slide your front foot back and slightly behind your right foot so that your body twists toward the center line of the attack. With a slight jump, deliver a round kick, taking your right foot to your opponent's trunk or face. Block with your left hand. Move your body weight forward in a fake. When your opponent starts to turn, shift your weight to your rear leg and rotate your upper body in the air. Lean back with your hips rolled forward for the round kick. Another option is to shuffle back with both feet and deliver a rear round kick or double round kick.

Counterattack 2

Your opponent attacks with a spin back kick. Execute a hop-step cut kick, taking your left foot to your opponent's trunk or ribs, and then perform a rear round kick, right foot to opponent's trunk or face.

Stand ready in open stance. Feint a low or a low and middle cut kick with your front foot. You may need to rechamber once or twice to start the attack. As your opponent starts to turn for the spin back kick, cut kick again to the rib or hip area (figure 11.34a). It is important to aim accurately; if the cut kick is off to the left, your opponent's rotation will cause the cut kick to spin off to the side. Aim the cut kick more to the right hip or ribs to stop the motion. Immediately follow up with a double round kick starting with either leg (figure 11.34b).

A different approach is to switch to a closed stance and fake with a rear cut. This fake is good for drawing a back kick. The same sequence follows once your opponent starts the spin back kick. As the rear cut kick comes forward, your opponent may be expecting a round kick. Instead use the cut kick to stop your opponent and then deliver a scoring kick. Usually your body weight will shift to your rear foot for the cut kick. Lean your upper body slightly forward. Once you set your foot after the cut kick, your body is in a forward motion, like running, for the double round kick. Alternatively make it a double round

a *b*

Figure 11.34 Counterattack to a spin back kick: *(a)* cut kick to opponent's hip to stop his rotation; *(b)* finish with a double round kick.

kick after the cut kick, taking your right foot to your opponent's trunk and your left foot to your opponent's trunk or face.

Counterattack 3

Your opponent attacks with a spin back kick. Counterattack by switching feet and executing a double cut kick (one low and one high) followed by a rear round kick.

Begin in ready stance. When your opponent starts the rotation, lean back on your right foot and, at the same time, lift your left foot off the ground in a cut motion. Hesitate at the low range and immediately plant another cut kick in your opponent's hip or ribs to stop his rotation. With a slight jump, follow up with a rear round kick to the trunk or face. Alternatively double the round kick with the second kick, taking your left foot to your opponent's trunk or face.

Counterattack 4

Your opponent attacks with a spin back kick. Counter with a rechamber step and a rear round kick, taking your right foot to your opponent's trunk or face.

Begin in ready stance. Use a low hop front cut kick to start the attack. As your opponent starts to rotate, rechamber the cut kick back far enough to avoid being hit by your opponent's back kick (figure 11.35*a*). As soon as your opponent's leg comes around for the kick, execute a round kick with the right leg, targeting your opponent's trunk or face (figure 11.35*b*). Shift your body weight forward to power your right leg for the round kick.

a   *b*

Figure 11.35 Counterattack to a spin back kick: *(a)* after hop front cut kick, shuffle back to avoid opponent's kick; *(b)* follow with a round kick to opponent's trunk.

Counterattack 5

Your opponent attacks with a spin back kick. Counterattack with a right round kick, taking your right foot to your opponent's trunk or face.

Begin in ready open stance. As a fake, switch your stance to closed and then move your left foot forward as if to round kick. Instead of executing a full round kick, plant your left foot where your right foot was and slide your right foot back and slightly off to the right (figure 11.36). You are now in an open stance. Execute a rear round kick from that position or pull your front foot to the rear, twist toward your opponent, and deliver a round kick with your right

Figure 11.36 Counterattack to a spin back kick. Shift from an open ready stance to a closed stance to an open stance with your right foot back and slightly to the right.

foot. The timing is the same—as your opponent rotates and starts to finish the back kick, deliver the rear round kick to your opponent's trunk or face.

Counterattack 6

Your opponent attacks with a spin back kick. Counter with a double round kick. Step back and 45 degrees to the right with both feet when you launch the kick. Take your right foot to your opponent's trunk and your left foot to the trunk or face.

Fake forward to draw in your opponent for the attack. As your opponent rotates for the spin back kick, slide your rear foot and then front foot back and 45 degrees to the side, out of the way of your opponent's kick. When your opponent's leg is fully extended or is dropping, execute a double round kick, first to your opponent's trunk and then to the trunk or face. Shift your body weight forward for the fake as if to attack. As you move back, keep your body slightly forward and use the power generated from your rear foot to launch the round kick. When shifting your position, the rear foot sets the direction of the body and the front foot slides back in the same direction. As an option, try a single rear round kick instead of a double.

Counterattack 7

Your opponent attacks with a spin back kick. Counter with a spin hook kick to your opponent's trunk or face.

Use your whole body to fake a front attack. As your opponent begins to rotate, step back 45 degrees to the right with your rear foot to avoid the kick. As his kick begins to drop, immediately pivot into a spin hook kick to the face (figure 11.37). Bend at the waist to get height on the kick. Other options

a   *b*

Figure 11.37 Counterattack to a spin back kick: *(a)* opponent's kick begins to drop; *(b)* pivot and execute a spin hook kick to your opponent's face.

include a spin back kick or jump spin back kick, a fast-step front round kick, or a hop-step front axe kick.

OPPONENT ATTACKS WITH A SPIN HOOK KICK

The spin hook kick is often used as a counterattack and can be very dangerous. Timing is integral to the technique. In this case, we are talking about how to counter an opponent who uses a spin hook kick as an attack strategy.

Counterattack 1

Your opponent attacks with a spin hook kick. Without stepping, execute a right-foot round kick to your opponent's trunk.

Use a strong fake, moving forward and perhaps trying a front-leg fake forward as if to kick. Once your opponent starts to spin for the hook kick, lean back and out of range (figure 11.38a). You want to be in position to execute the rear round kick as soon as your opponent's kick passes your face. Deliver the round kick to the trunk or face (figure 11.38b). Shift your weight to your rear foot and lean back to avoid your opponent's kick. Time it so that you deliver the round kick as soon as your opponent rotates past your face. Shift your weight forward. If your opponent's rotation is complete and she is starting to rechamber, your kick is going to land on her backside.

a   b

Figure 11.38   Counterattack for a spin hook kick: *(a)* lean back away from opponent's kick; *(b)* be ready to immediately execute a rear round kick once your opponent's kick passes your face.

Counterattack 2

Your opponent attacks with a spin hook kick. Counter with a rear-leg round kick (bada chagi), using a twist step.

Motion forward with your left leg in a fake. Once your opponent starts to rotate for the spin hook kick, slide your front foot back to your right foot, shift your weight, and kick with your right foot while your opponent is in an open stance and finishing the kick. Keep your weight forward during the fake but lean your upper body back to avoid being hit by your opponent's kick. Once the front leg slides back, your weight is on the left leg to support the right-leg round kick. Rotate your hips and, with a slight jump, deliver the round kick to the trunk. Another option is to shuffle back slightly with both feet and execute a rear round kick or double round kick.

Figure 11.39 Counterattack to a spin hook kick. As opponent starts to rotate for the kick, step straight back without pivoting.

Counterattack 3

Your opponent attacks with a spin hook kick. Counter by taking one step straight back or 45 degrees to the side with your front foot and executing a rear round kick.

Fake forward with your left foot to draw in your opponent. Wait for your opponent to bring his body completely around. As your opponent begins his rotation, slide your front foot straight back without pivoting (figure 11.39). Wait until the hook kick passes your face and then deliver a round kick, taking your left leg to your opponent's trunk or face. Shift your body weight to the side when the front foot moves to the back. Power the round kick forward off your left leg. A double round kick in place or a long spin back kick could also be used.

Counterattack 4

Your opponent attacks with a spin hook kick. To counter, take your rear foot straight back or 45 degrees to the right and attack with a right foot round kick to the trunk or face.

Fake forward with your left foot to draw in your opponent. As your opponent rotates around for the spin hook kick, you can either slide your right foot straight back or 45 degrees to the side to avoid the kick. When your opponent's kick begins to drop, launch forward off the right foot for a round kick to the trunk or face. Alternatively, try a double round kick with or without a slight jump, taking your right foot to your opponent's trunk and your left foot to his trunk or face.

Counterattack 5

Your opponent attacks with a spin hook kick. Counter with a tornado kick.

Watch for your opponent to start her rotation. As she is turning, shuffle back with both feet to get out of the way. Pivot on both feet to turn the body to the rear. As your opponent finishes the spin hook kick and her leg passes the middle point, pivot forward toward your opponent with your right leg lifted for the jump round kick. Your opponent should be just about at her beginning stance when you deliver the left-leg round kick.

Counterattack 6

Your opponent attacks with a spin hook kick. Counter with a low to high cut kick and a double round kick.

Switch your feet and change your stance. This move should entice your opponent to try a spin hook kick. As he rotates, cut kick low then high to stop his rotation and shift his balance. Rechamber by dropping your foot. Follow up with a double round kick, with or without a jump, taking your right foot to your opponent's trunk and your left foot to his trunk or face. Another option is to follow with a single round kick after the cut kick, or you can execute a hop-step front cut kick with a rear round kick, taking your right foot to your opponent's trunk or face.

Counterattack 7

Your opponent attacks with a spin hook kick. Counter with an in-place spin hook kick.

Use your entire body to feint, shifting your weight to your front foot. When your opponent begins to execute a spin hook kick, shift back and lean back so his kick misses. As the kick begins to drop, pivot and execute a spin hook kick to your opponent's face.

OPPONENT ATTACKS WITH A CLINCH

A clinch can be part of sparring strategy in a variety of situations. When your opponent attacks, you can counter with a clinch. When you attack, your opponent may try to clinch. Both of you might kick at the same time and end in a clinch. Punching and combination techniques can dissolve the clinch. Usually the fist attack is used at close distances to stop forward motion or to push the opponent forward to gain some space for the combination attack.

Counterattack 1

You and your opponent are in a clinch. Counter with a crescent kick.

If your opponent is performing a rear round kick, slide forward to clinch with a right-handed punch to the chest (figure 11.40a). Immediately deliver a rear-leg crescent kick to the face (figure 11.40b). If you attempt a fast kick and

a   *b*

Figure 11.40   Counterattack for a clinch: *(a)* counter a rear round kick by moving toward opponent to clinch and punching with your right hand; *(b)* follow through with a rear-leg crescent
kick to his face.

your opponent moves in for the clinch, you can use the same strategy. Punch
to your opponent's chest and then deliver a crescent kick to the head. The
punch is not for scoring but rather to stop your opponent's forward motion
and to control distance.

Counterattack 2

You and your opponent are in a
clinch. Counter with a jump spin
back kick or spin hook kick.

Let's say you move in with a
front-foot round kick and your
opponent immediately clinches.
Take the momentum of the contact and slightly push away from
your opponent with a right-handed
punch (figure 11.41). Slide your left
leg to the back and perform a spin
back kick or immediately jump
spin back kick upon contact. A
hook kick can be substituted.

When you attack with a rear
round kick and your opponent
moves in to clinch, use the momentum of the impact to shift your right leg
to the rear and immediately pivot to a spin back kick or spin hook kick.

Figure 11.41   Counterattack for a clinch. Use
a right-handed punch to push away from your
opponent.

Counterattack 3

You and your opponent are in a clinch. Counter with an axe kick or pushing kick, using your rear foot.

While in a clinch with your opponent, punch his chest. Keep your body weight on your front foot. Raise your right knee to your chest and execute a short, light axe kick, crescent kick, or pushing kick. You can add a slight jump to add distance or power.

Counterattack 4

You and your opponent are in a clinch. Counter with a front-foot arc and round kick or double round kick.

When your opponent starts to back out of the clinch, seize the opening to attack with any combination of kicks. If necessary, you could circle with either foot, clockwise or counterclockwise, to open up the clinch for your kick. Or you could try taking one step back to release the clinch and immediately launch a single or double round kick.

Counterattack 5

You and your opponent are in a clinch. Counter with a rear round kick and spin hook combination.

Let's say you attacked with a rear round kick and your opponent moved in to clinch. Quickly rechamber your kicking leg, pivot, and send a spin hook kick to his face (figure 11.42). A double round kick would also work, or try rechambering and immediately executing a jump spin back kick.

Counterattack 6

You and your opponent are in a clinch. Counter with a block, punch, and rear axe kick or crescent kick to your opponent's face.

Your opponent attacks with a spin back kick and you move left and forward at a 45-degree angle to clinch. In the clinch, block your opponent's rotation with a right-handed block to the back of the leg and a left-handed punch to the ribs (figure 11.43). Be careful not to punch the spine; this will result in a penalty from the judges. Immediately, deliver a rear-leg (right-leg) crescent or axe kick to the face.

If your opponent attacks with a front cut kick, again block, this time with the left arm. Punch to the ribs with your right hand and execute a rear-leg axe kick to the head. Remember the top and sides of the head are fair game; the back of the head is penalty territory.

a

b

c

Figure 11.42 Counterattack for a clinch: (a) opponent interrupts your kick by clinching; (b) rechamber your kicking leg and step away; (c) pivot and execute a spin hook kick to his face.

Figure 11.43 Counterattack for a clinch. If opponent attacks with a spin back kick, move in to clinch. Block your opponent's leg with your right hand and punch him in the ribs with your left hand.

Counterattack 7

You and your opponent are in a clinch. Counter with a rear-foot round kick.

In the clinch, you and your opponent both have your left foot forward. You can either swing your left foot in an arc to the rear (like a half-circle motion) and then round kick with that same foot (figure 11.44) or you can swing your right rear foot in an arc to the right and rear for a right-foot round kick. When bodies collide, there is forward momentum in the clinch. Use that body contact to manipulate your opponent's position for your counter with the round kick, in effect moving your opponent back to create distance for the kick.

a   *b*

Figure 11.44   Counterattack for a clinch: *(a)* back out of the clinch by moving foot in a half-circle; *(b)* use the right leg to round kick to the trunk.

12

Making Weight

The loss, gain, and maintenance of body weight is a topic that has been tackled on many fronts. Doctors, dieticians, and scientists all have had their say on the hows and whys of weight control. Many sports, including taekwondo, divide athletes into weight classes or divisions to provide a fairer contest, which means weight is a vital factor in the match. Athletes of all weight classes who participate in local or international matches must deal with weight control.

You should address weight control as part of your total training plan and approach it in a systematic manner. An athlete's weight within a weight division is directly linked to ability to perform during a match. For this reason, athletes are liable to experience a great deal of stress in trying to make weight.

Athletes should include weight control in their preparation for a match. Most athletes in the lightweight division are trying to reduce their weight. At the other end of the weight classes, athletes in the welterweight, lightweight, and heavyweight divisions make weight by gaining weight.

In taekwondo, there are usually eight weight classes for males and four classes for females. Athletes might try to lose weight for many reasons. For example, they might wish to stay in a present weight class, to avoid a match against an outstanding athlete in the same weight class, or to improve their ability to perform by being in good condition. Athletes who successfully control their weight while maximizing physical function for the match have a better chance for victory.

Past experiences with weight loss and current weight status will affect how much weight an athlete is capable of losing and how long it will take. On average, a juvenile athlete who is still growing may lose 2 to 4 pounds (1 to 2 kilograms) to make weight, while an adult may lose 2 to 7 pounds (1 to 3 kilograms). Some athletes lose their weight in a week or two. Some try to lose weight in three or four days, and when they fail to reach their goal, they may even try to reduce their weight by 2 to 3 pounds (1 to 1.5 kilograms) in a day.

Athletes use different methods to control their weight. Weight loss through regular exercise, dietary control, and moderate perspiration is the most common and healthy way to lose weight. Increasing body heat in a sauna or by wearing a rubber suit to remove fluid from the body through perspiration are two methods used by some athletes. Some athletes turn to pharmaceuticals such as diuretics and laxatives.

For rapid weight loss, the athlete must control food and beverage intake for at least three or four days before weigh-in and then increase body heat to cause water loss through sweat.

A long-term plan allows an athlete to gradually reduce weight by 2 to 3 pounds (1 to 1.5 kilograms) through regular exercise and dietary control. In that manner, the athlete maintains a stable, healthy condition and does not stress the body. Flexibility is improved as well as ability to perform in a match.

On the other hand, athletes who attempt unreasonable weight loss within a short period may experience symptoms such as anemia, fatigue, decreased motivation due to malnutrition, vomiting, bloating, and overall poor health. These health conditions can be directly linked to failure in a match.

In the past, weighing in for competition was done on the day of the match. As a result, athletes who rapidly lost weight were disadvantaged in the ring due to their diminished physical condition. Today athletes weigh in the day before the match so that they have time to recover lost fluids.

Considerable time is required for the body to return to its normal condition after rapid weight loss. The human body is 70 to 80 percent water and is very vulnerable to fluid loss. Quick weight loss is due to a loss of body fluids, which in turn can bring about indigestion and stomach trouble. Weight loss through dehydration is not desirable.

After the weigh-in, an athlete should replenish fluids. Many sport drinks help rapidly replenish carbohydrates and essential minerals. Water should be consumed at 10- to 20-minute intervals in such a manner that is not excessive and does not cause stomach malaise. Nutritional replacement via easily digestible foods or energy bars is also helpful. Energy bars are convenient and contain the necessary nutritional elements. If there is time, the athlete should take familiar foods.

The best weight control is part of a long-term plan. Set a reasonable target weight and reduce weight by exercising regularly and controlling the amount of food consumed. Base caloric intake on a weight-loss target and participate in regular exercise to burn fat calories. Instead of eating two or three big meals, consume food in several small meals throughout the day. Moderate, balanced consumption of the basic food groups is best; however, specific nutritional and health needs must be addressed on an individual basis. A good source of information for athletes is *Nancy Clark's Sports Nutrition Guidebook* (2003, Human Kinetics). Several countries also offer nutritional guidelines. In the United States, the most recent dietary guidelines can be found at www.mypyramid.gov. Health Canada offers nutritional information and guidelines at www.hc-sc.gc.ca, and the Wired for Health site of the United Kingdom, www.wiredforhealth.gov.uk/doc.php?docid=7267, also offers guidelines for a healthy diet.

Consuming carbohydrates before and after practice, after weigh-in, and before the match may increase the duration of exercise that the athlete can perform. Carbohydrates such as pasta, rice, and breads are converted to sugar, which generates energy. Moderate meals should be eaten three or four hours before a match.

It should be reiterated that weight loss through dehydration is unhealthy. It is important to incorporate a long-term, systematic plan that uses exercise and diet to achieve weight control and improve health. A healthy body is the foundation of performance and is an important factor in the realization of athletic goals.

13

Controlling the Match

If you were taking a journey, you would need to pack the proper clothing for your destination, know which airline you were taking and what time you were leaving, be familiar with the weight and size limits for luggage, and so on. Not having this information would interrupt the whole trip. Participating in a state, national, or international event is not much different from taking a journey. You need to collect key information so that you can plan accordingly. Three factors to consider when planning your match strategy are what pregame details you need to know, how to save energy in the match, and how to use feints to your advantage.

An old saying in real estate is "Location, location, location." When preparing for high-level competition, the equivalent saying is "Experience, experience, experience." Many factors shape a successful fighter. First, you must have the desire to train, persevere, and win. You must train extensively and train well. You must expose yourself to many arenas and competitors to build your repertoire of strategies. Experience builds your skills and your ability to read an opponent. The final quality is spiritual—the indomitable spirit. When the will is lacking, the spirit kicks in. When the spirit is lean, the will kicks in. Either way, your internal voice keeps you moving forward and the spirit grows as passion for the sport grows.

To save energy, you must know your opponent as opposed to attacking blindly and wasting movement. Many a match has been lost not because of poor technique but because of exhaustion. Overzealous fighters, pumped with anxiety, can attack the first round in a flurry of kicks. However, at the sound of the buzzer they are gasping for air and have already expended stored energy. This chapter discusses smart strategies that turn a street fighter into a fine-tuned winner.

Finally, fakes and footwork are an integral part of the match. I often refer to feint techniques as fishing, for that is what you are doing—fishing for a reaction, seeing what your opponent might do with your proposed intentions. This is where experience with different partners plays an important role. You cannot learn how to read an opponent from a manual. There are far too many visual clues that you must categorize, making it impossible to create a picture that is the same for each opponent. You must develop a keen sense of visual references that trigger automatic responses, because you can always throw your fishing line in the water, but that doesn't mean you'll catch anything.

GATHERING PREGAME DETAILS

All sports have regulations, and matches are held according to such rules. Game rules for local and international games usually are not the same. It is necessary to have a good understanding of regulations for a particular event in order to prepare for matches and formulate scoring strategies. Before starting a match, you should understand what tasks need to be carried out to ensure a smooth event. You must be able to adapt to changes, collect information before the match, and control your anxiety when participating in a competitive event.

Weather and other environmental conditions may affect your concentration on the day of the match. A large crowd, unfamiliar venue, or change in your competitive situation may be distractions. These problems can be overcome through mental training (see chapter 8).

Collect all the information you need before the match, such as schedules and match times. The athlete or coach needs to confirm which age and weight division is appropriate and the number of athletes participating in that group. If you have some free time before the match, observe the athletes in your age and weight class. Note each potential opponent's physical condition, match style (attack or defense), habitual motion patterns, and tactics. Armed with this information, conduct a mental match with the opponent using the opponent's own counterstrategies. This is a crucial process. When you know your opponent, you can take the field with confidence. Feedback about an opponent from fellow athletes or a coach is also effective.

Prepare for potential stress factors. If possible, stop thinking about situations that may cause apprehension, such as fear of a strong opponent, injury, or unfair calls by judges. Use visualization to mentally adjust to a strong opponent before the match. Imagine difficult situations you may encounter and mentally prepare countermeasures as you enjoy your mental match. Before the match, seek feedback from fellow athletes or coaches who have met your potential opponents in matches.

If you feel tension or anxiety before a match, listen to music, control your breathing, and establish psychological stability. About 30 minutes before the match, relax tense muscles and increase flexibility through stretching. Before and during the match, deeply inhale and exhale to relax the mind and body.

SAVING ENERGY

Good timing in attacks and counterattacks can help conserve energy. To improve your timing, carefully observe your opponent's posture, stance, distance, habitual movements, and feints to gain an understanding of your opponent's attack methods and rhythms. Using a variety of feints will create chances for attacks and induce attacks from the opponent. The more you know about your opponent, the better you will be able to time your attacks and counterattacks. It is important to develop the ability to read an opponent accurately. Make adjustments based on the information you learn about your opponent prior to the match.

Many athletes worry about where to fix their sight during the match. Should you look at your opponent's lower body in anticipation of a kicking attack? Should you watch the eyes to get a sense of her fighting style? These questions demonstrate the importance of sight during the match.

Line of sight can be classified into a central visual field and a peripheral visual field. These two types of vision work together. To an extent, where you choose to fix the central visual field is a matter of personal preference. Depending on the opponent, watch either the eyes or the attacking part of the lower body. Use your circumferential visual field to watch your opponent's movements. Excellent athletes have a well-developed circumferential visual field that they use to see opponents' movements that occur in the periphery. They read muscular changes, make instant judgments, and react accordingly.

Often beginners are unfamiliar with the importance of the circumferential visual field and depend too much on their central vision. These athletes will have a difficult time grasping the overall rhythm of the match. Through repetitive training under matchlike conditions, beginners can considerably improve their understanding of an opponent's reaction.

Watch the posture and motion of the opponent. Reading movement in this way will help you discover your opponent's weaknesses.

Mental concentration before the match should focus on the desire to win. Link this desire to positive actions in the ring. The duration of mental concentration is 10 seconds. Therefore, at 10-second intervals, alternate concentration and relaxation in order to foster self-control.

If you don't have the opportunity to observe your opponent before the match, you will need to collect information during the match. When the opponent is unknown, reckless attacks may cause you to lose points. Instead you should discover your opponent's reactive motions by using feints and steps. Analyze your opponent's reactions and use this information to appropriately attack and defend.

There are many ways to discover an opponent's reactive motions. By engaging in many practice drills with a number of partners, you will experience a variety of reactions, which will help you improve your ability to adapt to changing situations.

Your opponent's posture or stance will tell you many things about his fighting style. A difference in posture can be discerned by looking at the opponent's foot stance. This will help you distinguish between an attack style (figure 13.1*a*) and a counterattack style (figure 13.1*b*).

A fighter with an attacking style will often have the toes of both feet facing forward. Attack-style athletes require more motion than defense-style athletes. Because they concentrate on attacking, these athletes may be weak in counterattacking. Stop the opponent's attack with a front- or rear-foot cut kick without changing position, or avoid the attack by sidestepping it. Immediately attack the opponent's face with your front or back foot. Your speedy counter will most likely give you the upper hand in the match.

Although there are some individual differences, in general a counterattacker stands in a sparring stance with the front foot at a 45-degree angle to the front and the back foot at a 90- to 110-degree angle. Any reckless attack against a counterattacker will most likely be countered. Before attempting an attack, analyze your opponent's skill through feints and steps. Then carry out an attack with confidence and speed using the proper techniques.

a   *b*

Figure 13.1 *(a)* A fighter who prefers to attack will stand with both feet facing forward. *(b)* A fighter who prefers to counterattack will stand with the front foot at a 45-degree angle and the back foot at a 90- to 110-degree angle.

You can also detect an opponent's reaction by feinting attacks that use the entire body, including the hands and feet. You can also use a variety of steps—forward, backward, and to the side—to manipulate the attack.

Sparring is relative, characterized by automatic reaction to the opponent's continuous movement. Depending on the opponent's reaction to a variety of feints, you can create chances to attack or prepare for counterattacks.

An attacking type of athlete tends to concentrate solely on the attack, leading to numerous weaknesses in defense. Against this kind of opponent, the moment the opponent attacks is your best chance to counter. Without changing your position, attack the opponent's face with your front or back foot. If the opponent's initiative upsets your timing, you will need to make a snap judgment on whether or not to close in, move backward, or sidestep to create a chance to attack.

When the opponent attacks fast, move back. The best time to attack is when the opponent's attacking feet contact the ground. Such a moment should not be missed. If you stay in the same position or move back slightly when attacked, you run the risk of sustaining a continuous attack. Thus it is necessary to close in or move way back to create an opening for your attack.

An opponent who seems to pull back for a brief rest may be tired. If you see your opponent breathing hard, it is a good time to attack.

When you execute a feint against an opponent, you may see your opponent hesitate for a moment. This indicates that the opponent is not ready to attack or defend. Another moment to attack is when the opponent reveals frustration after an attempt of a special attack skill fails. As she wonders about what kind of attack to use next, take advantage of her hesitation to attack.

When fighters are at the limit of their physical strength, they may wish to give up the game completely. Their feet do not move at their will. This often happens with beginners. The score is the determining factor for your next move. If you are winning comfortably, it is not necessary to relentlessly go after your opponent for the sake of another point. However, if the score is tied or you are behind, you have no choice but to continue attacking in an attempt to score.

You can create an opening for an attack when your opponent changes posture or is at full extension or moving sideways during an attack. Observe your opponent's reaction to feints. With the proper attack technique, you can take control of the game.

If the opponent moves backward in reaction to your feint, he likely lacks confidence. Moving backward also hinders a stable posture, which means it is a good time to attack. Control the game by using the proper skills and steps.

USING FEINTS

Since sparring in taekwondo is relative to the opponent, feints are all the more effective when you concentrate on the movements of your sparring partner.

Feinting motions include attacks with the hands, feet, or entire body and the use of steps. Feinting momentarily disturbs the concentration of your opponent, creating a chance to attack.

Feinting can also be used to persuade an opponent to attack. When the opponent attacks and exposes a weakness, counterattack or attack with good timing in order to gain the authority in the match.

When it is not possible to discern the opponent's style by his posture, use various feinting motions—such as raising and lowering your front foot repetitively—and analyze your opponent's reaction. When you have a chance to attack, control the match by using the proper skills—varying speed; feinting with a short, fast running-step axe kick; executing a long or short cut kick; using a pushing kick motion; or stepping with the front or back foot. Or, use a back-foot feint, take one step forward, and at the same time using the same foot as an axis, move sideways and watch your opponent's reaction.

After gathering information on your opponent, decide whether or not to take the first attack or counterattack. You must select the proper method quickly to control the game. The success or failure of an attack depends on accurate analysis of your opponent and the use of proper skill and timing.

In taekwondo sparring, the attack continuously changes through the endless body movements of the contestants. A good attacking opportunity that is lost will not come again. Hesitation means the athlete is anxious. Trust the skills you are going to use. Stop thinking about the opponent's possible counterattack and prepare for an attack in an instant.

You must quickly decide what kind of attack to use based on your read of the opponent. Is she an offensive or defensive fighter? What kind of attack and defense skills will she use? Does she move backward, try to grab, or move sideways? After making these judgments, don't be conscious of your opponent's counterattack; instead, carry out a faster attack. If you hesitate while attacking, it is likely that your opponent's counterattack will come quickly. Feints are used as a way to gain control. Only fast steps and kicks are effective against attacks or counterattacks. An opponent skilled in counterattacks is unable to cope with a fast attacking athlete.

The desire to win creates a psychological energy. It increases motivation and suppresses excessive tension and excitement, thus sustaining a strong resolve to win. When the opponent's weakness is exposed, carry out a bold attack with your best timing, animal instinct, explosive power, and speed.

ATTACKING TACTICS

In this section, we will discuss tactics you can use in different situations in the ring. These observations come from years of experience as a world competitor and coach. You are unlikely to find this information in taekwondo manuals. This is the final piece of the puzzle, the destination of the athlete's journey. The athlete comes to the ring with training, experience, strategy, knowledge,

Know as much as you can about your opponent's fighting style before you enter the ring. Understanding how your opponent will attack enables you to plan ahead for counterattacks and feints.

and spirit. The scoring system and time limits will influence your actions in the ring, so you must come to the ring with a full plate of information.

• Controlling the game when you are near the limit line and driven to a corner. Athletes who are near a limit line or driven into a corner will feel pressure because they are extremely likely to get a warning or lose points. Even while exchanging skills, a warning is issued if a step crosses the limit line once or twice, increasing the athlete's psychological burden. In such cases, you must stay cool to maintain control of the game. Decide whether or not to move one step back and counterattack, move sideways, or close in when the opponent attacks and is not fooled by a feint.

When closing in, attempt to move to an advantageous position by changing positions with your opponent. Rotate while closing in with a front cut kick. Or, turn around and escape at a 45-degree angle while faking an attack with your back foot near the corner or limit line.

If the opponent makes a cut kick, stop the attack with a front-foot kick without changing position and attempt a continuous motion according to the circumstances. Or, close in simultaneously with a fist attack to the chest or a continuous attack and rotate, pivot, and escape.

When a good opening for an attack occurs, assertively attempt a pushing kick, tornado kick, tornado with a double round kick, or back kick.

• Controlling the game when your opponent is driven to the limit line. Opponents feel the same psychological burden you do when driven to a corner or limit line. By feinting and taking steps, carefully judge whether or not your opponent will attack, defend, or close in. If your opponent is inactive, she is waiting for an attack. Make a safe, confident, and bold attack. Induce your opponent to receive a warning by pushing her outside the limit line with a cut kick or with a front- or back-foot pushing kick. Or, use continuous motion by means of a cut kick and pushing kick to gain dominance. If you and your opponent are exchanging techniques when your opponent is pushed out of the ring, most likely the referees will not issue a warning. However, if the opponent is backing up and not countering your attack, she will get a warning and a half-point deduction.

• Controlling the game when losing by a slight difference in score. When your opponent is winning, he may attempt a half-hearted attack while moving backward or forward. If you get nervous and attempt a reckless attack, defeat may be imminent. Suppress your excitement and control the game with cool assurance. Drive your opponent to a corner or limit line with a cut kick, front- or back-foot pushing kick, or jump pushing kick. Boldly attempt a continuous attack to your opponent's face with a double round kick, spin back kick, or running-step down axe kick. Another possibility to control the game is to induce your opponent to do something to provoke a warning that may add up to point deductions.

• Managing the score 20 seconds before the final round. Often when the second or third round is about to end, the positions of winner and loser are reversed. If you can earn 2 points for a face attack or an additional point for a standing-down or knockdown, you can make 3 points in a flash. With the 1, 2, 3 point system, you must never let your guard down. Carelessness, excitement, and inactive game performance all lead to warnings or loss of points, which lead to losing the match.

Maintain a proper level of tension and focus, performing your best until the end of the round. Ruffle your opponent with feint motions, footwork, cut kicks, pushing kicks, and running-step down axe kicks in continuous motion. Stop your opponent's attack and then attack with a continuous motion of closing in and moving backward. Be aware of openings for attacks. Take advantage of weaknesses that are exposed when your opponent attacks. You must have coolness and self-confidence to control the game.

• Controlling the game when the score is equal. If the score is the same in the second or third round, then before the start of the final match or during the match you must induce a point deduction for your opponent so that a win may be declared by superiority. When the score is the same or when there is no score, the judges decide who performed better. The standard for such judgment includes the following factors in the following sequence of application:

1. Superiority in the game
2. Number of first attacks
3. Number of times skills were used
4. Number of times highly difficult skills were used
5. Manner in the game

In cases of a superiority decision, face attacks and counterattacks should be used to control the game. Make continuous bold attempts by attacking with cut kicks and pushing kicks and executing attacks against the opponent's face.

• Controlling the game after an injury during the match. Sometimes fighters injure their ankles and knees during taekwondo matches. Injury during the game produces a great psychological burden and is often a disadvantage.

At such a moment, the coach's role is critical. The coach must instill a sense of confidence in the athlete to prevent discouragement. If continuing the match is possible, place the injured leg in front. Agitate the opponent to induce frequent attacks. When the opponent gets excited and attacks, close in to the opponent with the injured leg raised. Consider a face block while closing in. When closing in, raise the injured leg in such a way as to lay it in front of the opponent's feet.

When the opponent moves back, attempt a short pushing axe kick or down axe kick to the face. If the opponent is skilled in double attack and defense while moving backward, close in and raise the injured leg slightly in expectation of a double attack. Induce the opponent to attack the lower half of your body, hopefully resulting in a warning or point deduction. Counter the opponent's attack with a cut kick with your injured leg and then close in and attempt a continuous attack to the opponent's face. Or, close in with the injured leg raised and attack with the fist while simultaneously attacking the face in continuous motion.

14

Winning With a Coach

To a fighter, a coach is a leader, the general when it's time to enter the ring and fight. The coach is also an assistant and manager who objectively analyzes the athlete's technical ability and makes adjustments to improve physical strength, technique, and tactics. A good coach keeps a finger on the psychological pulse of the athlete so that the fighter is mentally prepared as well.

It is the coach's responsibility to stay current with the latest match rules and regulations in case the training plan needs to be revised. It may be necessary to develop new techniques and tactics that conform to the most recent regulations.

Once the fighter has decided to participate in a particular event, the coach establishes a training goal for the match. The match plan includes a period for game preparation, a training period, and a finishing period. The coach must take into account the athlete's age and ability and include training for physical strength, technique, and tactics. Depending on the time available for training before the event, the coach creates daily, weekly, monthly, or annual schedules and then helps the athlete carry out the training strategy.

The coach is a motivator, encouraging the athlete to strive toward established goals. The coach should also be a leader who creates a family atmosphere for training and can help resolve conflicts among athletes. When specific taekwondo training is not scheduled, team games should be included to create a favorable climate among athletes while building physical strength. Training plans should be developed with care so as to stimulate the desire for practice.

A coach should have rich game experience and outstanding knowledge of game management and tactics. A coach should be able to instantly analyze strategy and the strengths and weaknesses of the opponent before or during the game. The coach should make prompt judgments of changes in game situations and provide responsive techniques and tactics to the athlete. Tactics provided to the athlete before the game and during rest hours should be precise so that the athlete can also make instant judgments during a match.

A coach should be interested and committed to each athlete under her care and should frequently talk with her athletes. The coach should be a counselor and sounding board, open and available to the athlete who is experiencing anxiety or conflicts in his personal life. A coach should become an assistant who can communicate with sincere and discrete words during a game so as to create a sense of psychological stability and confidence for the athlete.

A coach should have an interest in the health and weight of athletes and should advise them accordingly based on the short- or long-term training plan. In particular, three to four days before a game, the coach should pay special attention to an athlete's nutritional intake, caloric intake, weight control, and injury care. The coach must make sure the athlete goes into the ring in the best possible condition.

All of these characteristics are important, but it is trust and integrity that connect the coach with the athlete. The athlete must know in her heart that her coach will stand by her with knowledge, experience, integrity, and protection of her best interests.

RING COACH

The ring coach and the athlete are a team. Before the game, they have a common goal of excellent match performance. The ring coach has autonomous control over the actions and thoughts of the athlete who enters the ring. The coach is responsible for giving instructions on game tactics prior to and during the game through predetermined, discrete words and signals.

Before the start of the match, the ring coach collects and analyzes information on the other athletes in the same weight class while watching the games. Once the coach has evaluated potential opponents and explained the analysis to the athlete, counterstrategies should be discussed. The coach also needs to get a fix on the psychological condition of the athlete and provide inspiration and encouragement as needed.

After the first round, a clearer picture of the opponent's techniques will guide the discussion of strategy between the coach and athlete. The ring coach must clearly explain what he wants the athlete to do so that the athlete hears, sees, and understands the coach's directions. The coach may need to demonstrate the moves he is suggesting to make sure the athlete fully understands. When the round begins again, the coach can reiterate his directions with short, one-word commands. If the groundwork for the strategy was clearly laid, reinforcements such as "back kick" or "clinch" should get the message across.

GAME PREPARATION

The athlete and coach should consider diet and weight control at least two weeks before the game. This will provide enough time for athletes who are outside their required level to lose or gain weight to make a particular division. No athlete should attempt to lose weight two or three days before a game; rather, an athlete should be in a position to eat in a healthy manner so that the body can perform at optimal levels.

The last two weeks before a match is the finishing period. During this time, the coach should identify the athlete's strengths and weaknesses and prepare the athlete to use certain techniques and tactics in the match. Any shortcomings should be explained precisely, and the coach should provide instructions before the date of the match. Psychological readiness should be strengthened as well (see chapter 8).

Before the game, the coach should secure accommodations near the stadium and transportation to and from the stadium. At the stadium, the athlete will need a place to keep required consumables such as drinking water, snacks, and tape.

The day before the game, the coach should visit the stadium and collect general information so that the athlete can familiarize himself with the environment. If possible, the athlete should engage in light team exercise to help him adjust to the environment and temperature.

Once the athlete makes weight (usually the day before the game), it is time to rest and relax with activities such as light jogging, listening to music, or swimming.

Before leaving for the stadium, prepare an ice cooler. Be sure to take ice, ice packs, drinking water, and a towel. Since absorption of nutrition before and during the game is directly linked to performance, have emergency food on hand such as energy bars or fruit.

It is advisable to arrive at the stadium at least one hour before the game. This will give the athlete time to collect information and mentally adapt to the upcoming match. While watching the games, analyze and record information on potential opponents.

Before the game starts, tape those parts of the body that are subject to injury. Perform some warm-up exercises and stretches 30 to 40 minutes before the match to increase flexibility.

Immediately before the game, the coach should ascertain the psychological condition of the athlete and foster psychological stability and confidence. The athlete should practice deep breathing before the game to encourage relaxation and a calm state of mind. If the opponent's tactical strategies have been identified, the coach and athlete should discuss the opponent's strengths and weaknesses. The coach should offer one or two specific counterstrategies. If the opponent's tactics have not been identified, the coach should remind the athlete how to analyze the opponent during the first round. Then the coach should present strategies for scoring and counterattacks.

During the game, the coach should identify and analyze the opponent's tactics, strengths, and shortcomings. The coach should also identify the tactics, strengths, and shortcomings of his own athlete. If the athlete has a problem with game management during the match, the athlete's attention should be directed more often to the coach. If the athlete does not use the tactics as instructed by the coach, the coach should emphasize the importance of the tactics with words and hand signals.

Strategies often change during a game in response to the opponent's tactics. The athlete and coach should use short words and hand signals to communicate these changes.

If an athlete sustains an injury during the game, a decision should be made whether or not to continue or abandon the game. Taekwondo rules for sparring include time limits for injuries. Usually there is one minute for a review from a team physician for a nonserious injury. If the injured athlete does not recover after a count of 8 by the referee, then the WTF competition rules of articles 18 and 19 apply. That's the simple explanation.

However, other circumstances, such as the athlete's personality, the event, and the athlete's future in the sport, may come into play. One example that comes to mind is a collegiate event that I coached in Taiwan. In the first round, the score was 4 to 2 in favor of my athlete. After the second round, the score was 7 to 2 in my fighter's favor, but his knee had started to act up. In the third round, the athlete hyperextended his knee. After he was examined by

Even the best plans may change during a match. Communication between fighter and coach will ensure that the fighter has the best chance of overcoming the unexpected.

the physician, the consensus was that my athlete could continue if he wanted; however, the doctor's recommendation was 70 percent that the athlete should not continue. The athlete was winning by a comfortable margin but would lose if he quit. In view of the athlete's long-term goals, I determined that he should throw in the towel to signal that he was giving up and accepting disqualification. If he had persisted and won the fight, he would have gone on to a semifinal match and possibly intensified the injury. This was not in the athlete's best interest, as it was important that he maintain the integrity of his knee for the future. Sometimes the coach has to make that call to protect the athlete.

If the situation were different, for example if it were the last major event in the fighter's career, then maybe the athlete and coach would agree to continue the match with the concurrence of the referee. In any case, a number of factors influence the decision to continue or withdraw after an injury.

During the intermission between each round, the coach should be on hand with a cold drink of water and a cold towel so the athlete can wipe off sweat. The coach should take this time to praise good performance and instruct the athlete on new tactics based on analysis of the opponent.

If an athlete fails to follow tactics as instructed by the coach, the coach should not rebuke her. Instead the coach should emphasize the importance of the tactics and repeat the instructions. The coach needs to remember the athlete's abilities when providing tactical instruction. The coach should use short, accurate words to give precise points of instruction and should explain the opponent's tactics through gestures, demonstration, or face-to-face communication with the athlete.

An athlete who sustains an injury during the game may feel psychologically unable to continue. The coach needs to instill psychological stability and confidence and reinforce the athlete's willpower. Depending on the severity of the injury, the coach should instruct the athlete on specific methods of attack and counterattack to avoid further injury. The score at the end of each round may directly affect the technical strategies used. If the athlete is winning by a comfortable margin, then a stall might be employed. If the match is tied, then the timing of a scoring attack is the concern. If the athlete is down in points, then particular attacks or counterattacks that do not aggravate the injury should be applied.

The coach needs to remind the athlete not to get too excited and to pay attention to the scoring and maintain a proper level of tension and concentration through the end of each round. Before each round, the coach should remind the athlete to take deep breaths to relieve tension and relax contracted muscles.

Regardless of the outcome of the game, the coach needs to praise the athlete and instill a sense of confidence. The coach and athlete need to analyze the match, focusing on ways to improve the athlete's weaknesses and showcase the athlete's strengths for the next event. They should set new goals to motivate the athlete for the next game.

COACH–ATHLETE COMMUNICATION DURING THE GAME

Success in the ring requires athletes and coaches to communicate tactics using hand signals and words based on accurate data. Smooth communication requires frequent and repeated training. The coach and athlete can communicate with words, hand signals, and direct demonstration.

Improper communication before and during the game can have a negative psychological effect on the athlete. The coach should always encourage the athlete to cope positively with game situations. Since the coach's every word has a psychological effect on the athlete, discrete and specific communication is essential. The coach can influence the athlete's level of tension through his words. The following examples demonstrate how the coach's words influence the athlete's psychological condition.

- "Your contestant has rich experience in international games, so be careful." These words create excessive tension and excitement, lowering the athlete's performance rather than instilling confidence. It would be more prudent for the coach not to bring up this fact at all.

- "Be careful not to get hit." This comment is common in ring management, but it implies a lack of confidence in the athlete. The athlete may become focused on avoiding failure rather than winning. The coach needs to be more specific, perhaps suggesting a certain kick to watch for and how to counter it.

- "Be more alert." The coach should perhaps reiterate that the athlete needs to focus on the opponent as opposed to others outside the ring.

- "When you fight against the opponent, be more careful." Again, the coach needs to be more specific. The athlete should be careful about what? A spin kick? A jump kick?

- "Your opponent has a lot of game experience and has very good technique." Emphasizing the opponent's strong points without providing effective counters may cause fear and confusion. The athlete may feel unable to judge the situation or ascertain information about the opponent's tactics, making the athlete unsure of how to proceed. If an opponent has a specialty, then the coach should also provide a valid counterstrategy.

- "You will win against that opponent without any difficulty." These words may create confidence in the beginning, but if the opponent is more skilled than expected and the game turns unfavorably, the athlete may become flustered. It might be better to approach this situation as if both athletes were of the same caliber. Then the coach can focus the athlete on using what she has learned in training and doing the best job possible. After the first round, more specific strategies can be offered.

An excellent coach will use clear words to achieve successful results. The coach must precisely identify the opponent's tactics and communicate one or two specific counters to provide practical help. The coach should demonstrate his intentions with abbreviated taekwondo motions. A coach who wants an athlete to block with his left leg and kick with his right leg should grab the athlete's left sleeve and pat his right leg to make the instructions absolutely clear. Because of the noise level in the arena, a physical demonstration makes instructions more clear.

Words should be terse, specific, and precise. During the short breaks between rounds, the coach should remind the athlete of previous communication or change the tactics. Also, the coach should explain the opponent's strong points and shortcomings. The following statements are examples of specific, brief, positive instructions that will help the athlete in the ring:

- "Well done! The rear-foot round kick was slightly short. Make your kick longer."
- "After attack, don't retreat backward but close in. Link it to face by half-moon kick."
- "Don't retreat. When opponent makes a move to attack you with a rear-foot kick, stand still and cover yourself with left hand and counter-kick."
- "Be calm and do it as you did it in practice."
- "Opponent is very weak in rear-foot kick. Change your stance and attack with rear-foot kick at the same time."
- "Watch the electric sign from time to time. When opponent begins attacking in a highly excited condition, don't get excited but cope with it calmly."
- "Opponent mainly attacks by rear-foot round kick. With rear foot make attack motion. When opponent moves to attack, make front short axe kick while standing still."
- "Opponent is good in rear-foot kick. With your front foot, make a short offensive feinting motion. When opponent goes round, back off slightly and attack with round kick."
- "Opponent primarily carries out attack, counterattack, and round kick from one spot. At the spot where you stand, make motion for attack with rear foot and then attack by round kick and front-foot attack or running axe kick."
- "Opponent mainly uses short double round kick at the time of attack and round kick by rear foot as counterkick. You are faster. When opponent moves the rear foot for attack, attack with a jump spin back kick. At the same time move backward slightly and attack with a spin hook kick."

Sometimes a coach yells instructions to the athlete. This is an improper way to provide instruction. During the game, the athlete must concentrate on the opponent. Yelling can disrupt the athlete's concentration. An experienced coach knows how to make the most of brief opportunities to pass instruction with short words or hand signals. If the athlete does not use the instruction given, she needs to be reminded of the instruction.

For example, a fighter has just completed the first round and is with his coach. The fighter is breathing heavily and sweating, trying to regain his cool for the next round. His mind is churning with thoughts of the first round. The coach must get the fighter's attention and communicate appropriate strategies. A rambling discussion would be worthless; the coach must give short, specific directions to the fighter, including physical demonstrations. The athlete not only hears the coach, but sees and feels the coach's instructions.

Hand signals or short phrases make the most of given moments for communication. Information from coach to athlete should be based on the coach's judgment regarding the athlete's acceptance of such instruction and ability to process that information, which can vary among individuals. Coaches can achieve the common goal successfully by communicating with precise, accurate words, hand signals, and body gestures with legs and feet that convey the message. After training under the master for a long period of time, the athlete knows what the coach means by certain signals. It becomes an unwritten language between coach and athlete. Verbal communication is a little less reliable, especially if the fight is a good one and spectators are cheering. If the coach gets overzealous with directions to the athlete, he too can get a warning from the referee that affects the athlete's score. It has been my experience that in some cases an athlete is so focused on the match that he cannot hear the coach. In that case, the athlete must learn to watch for instruction from the coach.

Index

Note: The italicized *t* and *f* following page numbers refer to tables and figures, respectively.

About the Author

Master Yong Sup Kil is a seventh dan black belt, a four-time Korean national martial art champion (1973-1980), and the 1975 world champion. Since 1994, he has been coaching U.S. national teams, junior national teams, and U.S. national collegiate teams at World Tae Kwon Do championships. In 2000 Master Kil was named Coach of the Year by the United States Taekwondo Union, and he served as a United States Taekwondo Union (USTU) official delegate to the 2000 Olympic Games. In 2003, he represented the U.S. as a delegate to the Summer Universiade Games (World University Olympiad Games).

Master Kil holds the highest certificate in coaching (level 5) and has served on various United States Taekwondo Union (USTU) and USA Taekwondo (USAT) committees. He is a first-class international referee and acts as a special advisor and tactical trainer to law enforcement agencies. Currently, he is on the faculty in the department of physical education, Wayne State University in Detroit, Michigan. He has spent the last 10 years as chairman of the referee committee of the U.S. National Collegiate Taekwondo Association. Master Kil also operates Kil's Tae Kwon Do Inc. in Brighton, MI. Kil's Tae Kwon Do operates nine locations in Southeastern Michigan featuring competitive Taekwondo training and can be reached on line at www.kilstkd.com.

Complete Conditioning for

MARTIAL ARTS

SEAN COCHRAN

ISBN 0-7360-0250-2 • 184 pages

Complete Conditioning for Martial Arts is the most comprehensive resource for preparing the body to excel in karate, taekwondo, judo, aikido, jujitsu, kempo, and other martial arts forms. Loaded with exercises designed specifically to improve the execution of martial art techniques, this book supplies the workout prescriptions you need to excel as a martial artist.

Written by certified strength and conditioning specialist and black belt holder Sean Cochran, this book combines his expertise in both disciplines into one outstanding and widely applicable resource.

Develop the fundamental fitness and art-specific conditioning needed to master your discipline. With *Complete Conditioning for Martial Arts*, you'll always be in peak form.

To place your order, U.S. customers call TOLL FREE
1-800-747-4457
In Canada call **1-800-465-7301** • In Australia call **(08) 8277 1555**
In New Zealand call **(09) 448 1207** • In Europe call **+44 (0) 113 255 5665**
or visit **www.HumanKinetics.com**

HUMAN KINETICS
The Premier Publisher for Sports & Fitness
P.O. Box 5076, Champaign, IL 61825-5076